D0773177

DISCARD

The Society of the Poem

Modern poetry has never presented a more confused front of schools and movements, of revolutions and reactions than it does today. This new book, by a leading young English critic, is a searching exploration of the state of contemporary verse. Mr Raban combines a broad and expert knowledge of both English and American writing with a talent for hard-hitting argument, a sharp wit, and a discriminating personal taste. He argues that we can only understand the ideological battle-ground of today's literature by seeing it within the total context of the strains and tensions of contemporary society.

The Society of the Poem looks at society through its verse, and at poetry through the society in which it is being written. Mr Raban has sharp things to say about the current gurus of the day like Herbert Marcuse and Marshall McLuhan; at the same time he presents lucid and incisive critical readings of the works of poets as different as Philip Larkin, the American Black Mountaineers, the Liverpool pop poets, Ted Hughes, Robert Lowell, and many others.

This is a book which, because of its clarity, readability, and intelligence will be studied and talked about wherever contemporary poetry is read and valued.

Jonathan Raban

the society of the
poem

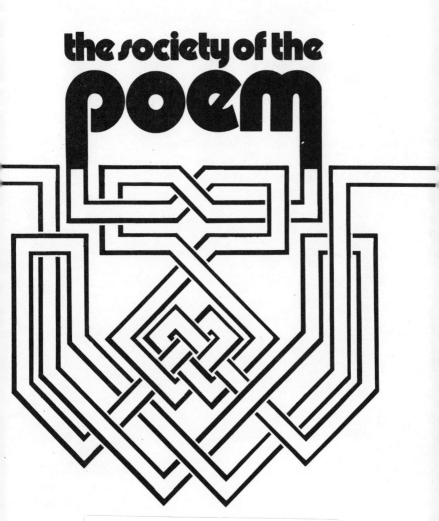

Distributed in the United States by
CRANE, RUSSAK & COMPANY, INC.
347 Madison Avenue
New York, New York 10017

First published in Great Britain 1971
by GEORGE G. HARRAP & CO. LTD
182-184 High Holborn, London WC1V 7AX

© *Jonathan Raban* 1971
Copyright. All rights reserved.

ISBN 0 245 50799 X (boards)
ISBN 0 245 50800 7 (paperback)

**Disbritubed in the United States by
CRANE, RUSSAK & COMPANY, INC.
52 Vanderbilt Avenue
New York, New York 10017**

*Composed in Monophoto Apollo type and printed by
Redwood Press Ltd., Trowbridge and London
Made in Great Britain*

Personal Acknowledgments

Some chapters of this book were broadcast, in abbreviated form, as talks on B.B.C. Radio 3 under the general title 'The Society of the Poem'. Chapter 8, 'A Place Not Our Own', appeared in *The Review*. I would specially like to thank George MacBeth, who read the manuscript and raised a large number of helpful queries, as well as pointing out some howlers. I'm also most grateful to Anthony Thwaite and Ian Hamilton, with whom I've been able to discuss particular parts of the book, and to Angela Lambert, who kindly read it in proof. To Francesca Greenoak, of Harrap, many thanks; the book started in conversation with her, and was sustained by her patience, interest and generous criticism; also to Lorna Sage, with whom I've argued out almost everything in the book, and without whom it would have been even more unscrupulous than it is.

I should also, sadly, like to thank the late Gerard Bell of Harrap who meticulously edited my manuscript. This was the last book he worked on before his sudden death; on behalf of all those authors whose books he read with such care and criticized so tactfully, may I record my own appreciation of his work. To the reader, it will be invisible, but the publisher and the writer can see Mr Bell's scrupulous attention to detail on almost every page.

J.R.

LONDON
November 1970–*May* 1971

The Society of the Poem

1

After Prufrock: The Poem and its Language

I'd been out the night before & hadn't seen the papers
    or the telly
& the next day in a cafe someone told me you were dead
And it was as if a favourite distant uncle had died
Old hands in the bigstrange room/new shiny presents at
    Christmas
and I didn't know what to feel.

ADRIAN HENRI, 'Poem in Memoriam T. S. Eliot'

It peeps slyly between the spaces left in the highbrow weeklies after the political articles, the reviews, and the advertisements have been set up in type; it rampages in public before huge audiences, sometimes to the sound of music; it is, in a British writer's phrase, 'a modest art'; it is used as a political weapon, to ban bombs and drive the American forces from Vietnam. The situation of contemporary verse is confused and contradictory; on the one side a battlefield, on the other a drawing-room, and both are strewn with old manifestos. The climate of technological change to which we've become accustomed is one in which cultural forms can spring up and as rapidly die as last year's de luxe Ford. A generation, as Leslie Fiedler is fond of remarking, now lasts for five years—at the last count. The stabilizing arts of language are both much sought after—as a culture we suffer a continuous need to explain ourselves to ourselves—and much despised; Marshall McLuhan assures us that we now live in a visual televerse, while Herbert Marcuse preaches that language has been so soiled by social experience that it can only enshrine archaic structures, and needs to be transcended.

Yet, despite the cross-fire in which it is situated, verse survives. It sells much better now than ten or twenty years ago; through television and the Albert Hall-style poetry jamboree it sometimes achieves a mass audience. It has, admittedly, a dishevelled, millennialist air, as if caught midway between two holocausts. It even wears an expression of thankful surprise, puzzled and gratified to have managed to get beyond the massive Stop sign of *The Waste Land*, of Pound's *Cantos*, of Yeats's burning and turning gyres. Eliot, in fact, has cast a long shadow over contemporary poetry; he has been The Bard of our century. 'Conformity' has meant keeping within the narrow lines imposed by Eliot on twentieth century verse, while 'radicalism' has entailed an equal acknowledgment of those lines, together with a commitment to diverge from them. Like Milton for an earlier age, Eliot is the Great Modern who has been miraculously transformed into our Only Ancient; mentor and yardstick, a forbidding folly, standing, like Ozymandias in the desert, to remind the traveller of the unwisdom of all sublunary poetic labours.

Eliot's habitual manner was that of a man carrying all his precious books down into his cellar, before putting on his gas-mask to await the inevitable coming of the barbarians. *The Waste Land* is, quite literally, a treasured library of European culture and learning, lovingly assembled and stored in suitably hermetic and hygienic conditions. There Dante and Shakespeare, the Elizabethan and Jacobean dramatists, Donne, Herbert, and the lyric poets of the seventeenth century, Pope, Dryden, and the French Symbolists all lie in their gleaming leather bindings, shoring up the ruins of that unmitigated disaster the twentieth century. The poem itself is a continuous, ironic exposition—phrased in exquisite pastiche and parody—of the unworkability of its own elitist, hierarchial values in a world of anarchical discontinuity. Its assertion of sensibility is simultaneously triumphant and doomed. Like all bardic epics (and, most specifically, like *Paradise Lost*), *The Waste Land* aspires to be the last poem that could be possibly written out of the wreckage of its own, dying civilization. Europe for Eliot, as Byzantium for Yeats, supplies an image of a culture whose death-throes are themselves the material for the highly wrought artifice of eternity. After *The Waste Land* only silence should have ensued—if only poets had the tact to follow Eliot's prescription. The trouble is that they very nearly did.

Eliot embodies very exactly a type of right-wing millennialism which has had an extraordinarily stable currency in salons, common-rooms, and lecture theatres since the 1920s. Spengler and Ortega y Gasset, with their happily twinning titles, *The Decline of the West* and *The Revolt of the Masses*, were the Jonahesque prophets of the movement. Novelists like Evelyn Waugh and Anthony Powell have been among its more unillusioned adherents—though in the work of both these writers the moral and social flexibility of the form of the novel has greatly tempered the totalitarian style of the doctrine. More recently Kingsley Amis and C. B. Cox and A. E. Dyson, the editors of the *Critical Quarterly* and the *Black Papers* on education, have revived the rhetoric with a remarkable degree of success, striking an Old Possum pose on matters of politics and poetry with such authority that, in academic circles at least, they sometimes seem to have ended the debate in a politely dull consensus.

To my mind the clearest, if metaphoric, statement of the Eliot position lies in *The Love Song of J. Alfred Prufrock*, which, on one level at least, can be read as a kind of encapsulated prophecy of the course of twentieth-century literary history. Of all Eliot's poems *Prufrock* comes nearest to laying out a personal programme, a Michelin route-guide to the territory ahead. Prufrock himself is a favourite figure in Eliot's pantheon of shabby characters, and crops up in many guises throughout Eliot's poetry—as Sweeney, for instance, and as Tiresias in *The Waste Land*. He is the last surviving poor relation of a once great culture, to be found by the time we reach him in the poem living off that culture's scraps, like a desiccated man of title reduced to a Bayswater bedsitter. During the course of the poem Eliot runs Prufrock through a gamut of possible literary and social styles, ironically testing each style, like an ill-fitting suit of clothes, against Prufrock's mangy figure. But, as the epigraph from Dante's *Inferno* implies, 'S'io credesse che mia riposta fosse . . .', this is a posthumous poem, spoken as a message from the dead: 'If I thought my answer was given to someone who could ever come back to the world, this flame would cease trembling; but since, if what I hear is true, no-one ever came back alive from this depth, I answer you without fear of infamy.'

Prufrock comprises the 'observations' (the subtitle of Eliot's first collection) of a cultural cadaver; it is the hollow voice of a twentieth-century corpse, fleetingly dressed in the finery of a dead civilization. And nothing fits. When Prufrock attempts the grand conceits of seventeenth-century verse in the first section of the poem—

> When the evening is spread out against the sky
> Like a patient etherized upon a table

—and in the tortuously extended cat/fog metaphor, we are primarily aware only of the inappropriateness of the gestures; these are languages which can no longer work. He flirts tentatively with the rhetoric of Swinburne and romantic decadence—

> I known the voices dying with a dying fall
> Beneath the music from a farther room.

He pokes at a more assertive style of realism—

> Shall I say, I have gone at dusk through narrow streets
> And watched the smoke that rises from the pipes
> Of lonely men in shirt-sleeves, leaning out of windows? . . .

but drops it abruptly in favour of a luxuriant pastiche of Baudelaire and French Symbolists:

> I should have been a pair of ragged claws
> Scuttling across the floors of silent seas.

He goes on to experiment with the waspish couplets of Pope, with a pseudo-biblical high style, with a rapid glance at the Jamesian novel, and comes temporarily to rest in that brilliant rhymed parody of a Shakespearian monologue:

> No! I am not Prince Hamlet, nor was meant to be;
> Am an attendant lord, one that will do
> To swell a progress, start a scene or two,
> Advise the prince; no doubt, an easy tool . . .

There is a superbly managed paradox here between the heroic posture of the tone and the craven statements it embodies; Prufrock, caught between his endless parade of literary guises, succeeds in being simultaneously tragic hero and fool. His heroism resides in the sheer poetic effort involved in his fool's odyssey in search of an appropriate style—an odyssey which culminates in a determined frivolity, phrased in the rhythms of tea-dance ragtime:

> I grow old . . . I grow old . . .
> I shall wear the bottoms of my trousers rolled.

Prufrock, like Pound's Mauberley, is an ironic model of the failed twentieth-century poet, of the writer who is the inheritor of many styles but for whom none is fully adequate. There is no single dominant language in the poem, so that each style is thrown into ironic relief by the existence of the others. Its structure is fragmentary and discontinuous; no rhythm or pattern of syntactical logic provides any ultimate shape or direction. And if we look for a containing dramatic situation to explain the existence of the poem we are rewarded with a conceit of such comic hyberbole that we have to reject it as absurd: *Prufrock* is a poem about a man trying to decide not to go in to a tea-party.

Yet one can't miss the air of millennial gloom with which

Eliot invests *Prufrock*; the sense that, in the figure of Prufrock, all available literary styles have been exhausted. The real metaphysical conceit behind the poem lies in the implication that it is an elegy, in the form of a footnote, to the death of Western culture. It's a conceit put with such ironical tact that it overtakes one by surprise; but it is unmissable. After *Prufrock* we are offered only frivolity, death, dreams, nostalgia; the fragmented relics of a culture which we may pick over, like the superstitious with their beads.

> We have lingered in the chambers of the sea
> By sea-girls wreathed with seaweed red and brown
> Till human voices wake us, and we drown.

The 'human voices', like 'the sound of horns and motors which shall bring/ Sweeney to Mrs Porter in the spring', are augurs of death—the death of tradition, of civilization, of literature, faced with the urgent discontinuity and disordered noise of modern life.

It's fair to observe, I think, that in all this doom and gloom Eliot does display a certain sentimental, American tourist's, affection for ruins; beneath the sophisticated and exquisitely manipulated ironies on the surface of all his work there runs a simple romantic relish for decay, as well as a taste for hellfire rhetoric of the It Is Later Than You Think kind. More importantly, the tradition at whose last rites he plays both priest and gravedigger is very much more limited and specific than the rhetoric of his verse might lead one to suppose.

It is, in fact, the tradition of assuming that the language of poetry is the most central and significant language of the culture; that the entire social, personal, intellectual, and professional life of a man can be contained within a single language at any one point in history. For Eliot the myth of the undissociated sensibility (which he explored with an almost archaeological nostalgia in his essay on Donne and the Metaphysicals) became inextricably entwined with the myth of Literature itself. His poetry is constantly scratching at the wound inflicted by historical circumstances on language; often shrill and hysterical in its demonstrations of the unworkability of traditional styles and patterns in a contemporary context. Even his cultivation, his well-bred ironical mask, has a quality of desperation. For he was never able to resist the spell of his conservative Eden; a world of craft, order, and stable religious structure, where language and literary tradition functioned as they might have done in a modern American's dream of seventeenth-century London or medieval Florence.

What is so puzzling is that Eliot's attitude—and the poetic style which it entailed—has passed into the common coinage of criticism, and poetry too, as the archetype of the modern in verse. For at almost every point Eliot played Canute to the forces of history. At a time when, in music and the visual arts, people like Picasso, Braque, Stravinsky, and Schöenberg were experimenting with forms and structures that would correspond to a human universe that was increasingly seen to be serial, technological, relativist, urban, Eliot devoted himself to a doomed, elegaic celebration of an irretrievable (and nostalgically mythicized) past. The 'newness' of his poetry was rooted in its ideology of heroic failure—in the Christian myth that in a fallen world the only poetry possible is a poetry that exhibits the scars of its divorce from the divine order.

It might be better to think of Eliot, not as the first great modern poet, but as the last writer at the end of an era. He has a good deal in common with those melancholy soothsayers of the nineteenth century, Arnold and Tennyson; in fact, in Tennyson's 'Locksley Hall Sixty Years After' we can hear the authentic accents of the waste land, stripped of Eliot's saving ironical grace and elliptical allusions:

> Tumble Nature heel o'er head, and, yelling with the yelling street,
> Set the feet above the brain and swear the brain is in the feet.

Bring the old dark ages back without the faith, without the
    hope,
Break the State, the Church, the Throne, and roll their ruins
    down the slope.

Authors—essayist, atheist, novelist, realist, rhymester, play
    your part,
Paint the mortal shame of nature with the living hues of Art.

Rip your brothers' vices open, strip your own foul passions
    bare;
Down with Reticence, down with Reverence—forward—
    naked—let them stare.

Feed the budding rose of boyhood with the drainage of your
    sewer;
Send the drain into the fountain, lest the stream should issue
    pure.

Set the maiden fancies wallowing in the troughs of Zolaism,—
Forward, forward, ay and backward, downward too into the
    abysm.

For both Eliot and Tennyson the notion of a full, explorable
poetic style was deeply tied to a disappearing social order,
and their verse was an act of salvage, rescuing those few
values that still remained from the engulfing chaos.

But as they wrote, the social structure itself moved further
and further away from the kind of idealized society created
within their poems. With the division of labour came a
corresponding division of language. As late as the 1870s
Matthew Arnold was able (with, admittedly, some rhetorical
strain) to write in the all-purpose language of the English
intellectual which he had inherited from Locke and Mill. The
philosopher/man of letters/social theorist/literary critic/
economist/public administrator were all able to function
within the same basic vocabulary and syntax. In Mill's style,
particularly, one can shift from sentence to sentence, even
from word to word, aware of the varying emphases of his
diverse interests; yet at no point do his roles become suffici-

ently autonomously defined to create any real tension. 'English' is one language, and 'literacy' is the ability to manipulate the whole language within the limitations imposed by shared social experience. Yet by the 1900s the characteristic style had become increasingly that of the specialist: the extraordinarily flat prose of the Webbs, which rivals the tone of a computer programme in its mathematical disambiguity; or the equally stylized rhetoric of the new popular journalism; or the stilted eloquence of political persuasion, magnificently exemplified in the oratory of Keir Hardie. During the twentieth century the language which we speak and write has lost almost all connection with that normative style in which politics and poetry, grocer's lists and military stratagems, drawing-room chat and legal proceedings, could happily coexist. Only in such rare dodos as the *Times* crossword puzzle can one find relics of the unified-language-in-a-unified-society which haunts Eliot's poetry like a tantalizing chimera.

During our own age the language of poetry has found itself hustled into the bazaar; it has become, at least in the eyes of the public, one of many professionalized rhetorics. In the late 1950s the Snow-Leavis debate in *The Spectator* about the 'Two Cultures' brought out into the open a series of issues which had been steadily festering for several decades. Quite aside from the guerrilla warfare, Cambridge style, which seemed to have been borrowed from one of the elaborate plots of Snow's own novels, the argument raised—and left unsatisfactorily answered—one central question: had literature, and the language of literature, so tied itself to a particular ideology (that of an essentially nineteenth-century liberal-humanitarian position) that it had doomed itself to fight on a single, narrow political-professional platform? One might observe that a depressingly affirmative answer was given by the way in which literary opinion, sensing that its professional status was under threat by the white-coated barbarians, tended to support Leavis in a show of industrial solidarity. Yet there is a strong argument to suggest—as Snow did—that Literature had become a profession in the worst sense. With the growing separation of jobs, languages, disciplines, Literature had come to define itself on the model of, say, the British Medical Association. Its contributions to party funds went to a kind of Gaitskellite liberal consensus of social democrats. Its code of general conduct included clauses governing such items as reverence for the past, distrust of newfangled things like science and technology, and a glum, nonconformist sort of piety towards the minutiae of private life. Poets should behave as far as possible like bank clerks, unless, like Dylan Thomas or Allen Ginsberg, they went the whole hog and set up in business as Bards. It was a code of conduct which resembled the contingency regulations enforced in disaster areas—a survival kit for inhabiting a waste land.

The public-relations journal for this depressed, embattled industry was Cox and Dyson's *Critical Quarterly*, a periodical which inherited a fair amount of the goodwill custom of Leavis's defunct *Scrutiny*; but it carried the gospel of the scrutineers with the tremulous faith of a lady missionary stranded, from pre-War days, in Maoist China. It defended Liberalism, moderate Christianity, and the regional voice; it turned a quizzical blind eye towards all poets, English and American, who smacked of any sort of radical experimentation. It championed the work of R. S. Thomas, Ted Hughes, and Philip Larkin, on terms which, in Hughes's case at any rate, seem profoundly inappropriate in the light of his subsequent development. The American poets whom the *Critical Quarterly* admitted into its cramped sanctum were Robert Lowell, Sylvia Plath, and Anne Sexton, on the thoroughly dubious grounds that they were 'confessional' writers, and therefore subscribed by proxy to liberal notions of the centrality of private life. Both the editors have subsequently become notorious in Britain for their role as whippers up of a right-wing, elitist backlash against the comprehensivization of education and student participation in the organization of universities. During the 1960s their conservative poetics were increasingly translated into broad political terms; it has been an entirely natural movement, and has dramatized, even parodied, the larger social implications of the liberal-conservative literary attitude. Exactly the same phenomenon has been observable amongst the American champions of Eliot, the New Critics; although in the case of Brooks, Tate, and Wimsatt the interweaving of poetics, Christian doctrine, and politics-at-large has been conducted with such subtlety that it has had the air of the conjuror's 'Now you see it; now you don't'.

All this would, indeed, be a hanging up of parochial dirty linen, were it not for the fact that the texture of so much contemporary verse itself seems to have absorbed the dogma, initiated by Eliot, maintained by both Leavis and the New Critics, and kept fitfully alight by the *Critical Quarterly* and its numerous academic admirers, that the twentieth century has forced poetry to acquire a particular, literary-political ideology. What has been most dramatically enforced has been the distinction between 'the poem' as a context—and all the traditional, liberal values with which it is supposedly associated—and its 'language', the discontinuous hubbub of a modern world in which 'the poem' has had to adopt a strategy of mandarin irony. It is a distinction whose importance it is impossible to over-emphasize—a distinction uniquely characteristic of twentieth-century verse. We can hear its beginnings in Browning's dramatic monologues, when the voices of Mr Sludge, Bishop Blougram, and Fra Lippo Lippi—all very much figures 'of the world', intrinsically anti-poetic in their slangy materialism—are incorporated, by sheer brute force, into a doggerel verse style which seems to be deliberately corrupted by the queer sort of persons it has to accommodate. In Eliot's work the distinction comes to have an insistent, nagging presence; in the 'Sweeney' poems, and in 'A Cooking Egg', a kind of racy vulgarity is maintained in the verse with the icy politeness of someone holding something nasty at the end of a pair of tongs:

> I shall not want Honour in Heaven
>> For I shall meet Sir Philip Sidney
> And have talk with Coriolanus
>> And other heroes of that kidney.

In *The Waste Land* this tendency reaches its apogee in the 'When Lil's husband got demobbed, I said—' section; where the verse, somewhat squeamishly, resolves to make ironic silk purses out of vulgar sow's ears:

> I didn't mince my words, I said to her myself,
> HURRY UP PLEASE IT'S TIME
> Now Albert's coming back, make yourself a bit smart.
> He'll want to know what you done with that money he gave you
> To get yourself some teeth. He did, I was there.
> You have them all out, Lil, and get a nice set,
> He said, I swear, I can't bear to look at you.
> And no more can't I, and think of poor Albert,
> He's been in the army four years, he wants a good time,
> And if you don't give it him, there's others will, I said

The poem itself operates as a context in which the disparate, often soiled languages to be found in it are defined, held up against all the traditional standards which the poem as a form implies. The working-class characters who are given voices in *The Waste Land*—the women in the pub, the bored typist, the cocky clerk, the girl who loses her virginity at Richmond on the floor of a narrow canoe—are made to stand on display like so many plebeian curiosities lined up in the morning-room of a London club. Look at Homer, look at Shakespeare, look at Dante . . . look at *these*. The details which accompany them, like the underwear and the tinned food in the typist's bed-sitter, are catalogued by Eliot with fascinated repellence. One shouldn't forget that it is by his invitation that they exist in the poem at all; for Eliot's basic strategy is to make us believe that these alien languages have somehow foisted themselves on to his verse, where they pollute the poetic tradition like maggots working away at a piece of carrion.

The ironic distance which Eliot puts between the poem and its language has carried as a major convention into recent verse, where it sometimes seems to exist as a kind of required nervous tic. What does one make, for instance, of the much-anthologized poem by Peter Porter, 'Your Attention Please'? It begins:

> The Polar DEW has just warned that
> A nuclear rocket strike of
> At least one thousand megatons
> Has been launched by the enemy
> Directly at our major cities.
> This announcement will take
> Two and a quarter minutes to make.
> You therefore have a further
> Eight and a quarter minutes
> To comply with the shelter
> Requirements published in the Civil
> Defence Code—section Atomic Attack.
> A specially shortened Mass
> Will be broadcast at the end
> Of this announcement—
> Protestant and Jewish services
> Will begin simultaneously—
> Select your wavelength immediately
> According to instructions
> In the Defence Code. Do not
> Take well-loved pets (including birds)
> Into your shelter—they will consume
> Fresh air. Leave the old and bed-
> ridden, you can do nothing for them . . .

Porter artfully courts his clichés and his officialese so that they take on the air of something *found* in the external world beyond the poem. They are made to look like the language of unpoetic (and the jump is a small one to *unhumane*) reality; though in fact the idiom of the poem belongs—however marginally—to science fiction. And Porter emphasizes this sense of an objectively actual language by deliberately

WHITWORTH COLLEGE LIBRARY
SPOKANE, WASH.

repressing all latent metrical patterns. Each line is made to end arbitrarily, so that although it looks like a poem, when one comes to read it one discovers that it has none of the rhythmical properties associated with lines that stop short of the end of the page. Its 'poetic' force lies in the quality of attention which we bring to its language. The 'poem' has become merely a context—a test-bed or wind-tunnel in which one particular, non-poetic idiom is subjected to scrutiny. Yet what happens is paradoxical in an oddly anarchic way. On one level the newspeak of overkill becomes more alarming; we are allowed, in the leisured, disinterested atmosphere of the context of the poem, to watch the dreadful banalities of cliché work in slow motion, to see the way in which the deadening jargon of the public-address system has already killed off human life long before the bombs have got to work. But on another (and I don't feel that Porter is sufficiently in control here) the language is de-fused, made harmless, simply by being 'in a poem'. The ease with which it can be randomly chopped up into verse units is some sort of worrying proof of its digestibility; the fine, considered liberal art of poetry can deal with nuclear strikes as smoothly as it deals with daffodils.

One could endlessly multiply examples to illustrate this technique and the inevitable tension it entails. Two will do. The first is from a poem by Christopher Middleton called 'Computer's Karl Marx', which is headed by a quotation from Bukharin, 'How does . . . this reorganization of production relations actually proceed . . . ?' Middleton answers the question by juxtaposing a series of nouns and verbs in a series which might be fed as a programme into a binary computer. My quotation is the second of three stanzas:

> conscript prostitutes
> rusticate prelates
> cut pop opiates
> stop past increments

    start national product
    poor labourers
    proud as lions
    note price reduction

The language of Middleton's poem is highly organized and inventive; its resemblance to a real computer programme is a matter of broad, stylized outline, achieved mainly by the removal of tacitly existing articles and prepositions. It has the verisimilitude of a sketch. But the poem's success—and Middleton is a writer of great intelligence and calculation—comes from the way in which this paradigmatic profile of a computer language works reflectively back, both against the concept of 'the poem' and against its hypothetical source in an electronic idiom. The wordy, metaphoric, rhythmical qualities associated with the notion 'poem' (and of which we're allowed a fleeting glimpse in the only simile in 'Computer's Karl Marx': 'proud as lions') are played off against the bare verbs and list of commodities and functions which compose this particular poem. It brings together, in a form as close to a metaphysical conceit as the twentieth century will allow, two conceptual worlds: the world of 'poetry', and all the values that are implicitly brought into play by the act of committing words to paper in a verse sequence, and the intensively active world of politics and economic transactions —a world stripped naked of elegant syntax, a world without metre, a world in which only the most functional adjectives are permitted.

    Finally, a poem by Robert Creeley. Called 'Hello', it finds its language in the folk-argot of the sex-and-violence thriller, and uses the metrical and typographical shape of the poem as a means of reconstituting a tired and predictable idiom into something altogether new and strangely dangerous:

    With a quick
    jump he caught
    the edge of

her eye and
it tore, down,
ripping. She

shuddered,
with the unexpected
assault, but

to his vantage
he held by
what flesh was left.

The first three stanzas keep the vocabulary of the original
almost entirely intact. Only the expected word 'dress' has
been changed to 'eye'; and the cliché phrasings have been
cunningly bisected by the line-endings. With these adjust-
ments the mechanically functional language of the thriller
assumes an equivocal significance: the struggle to articulate
the single short line—a continuing feature of all Creeley's
verse—becomes in this poem both a struggle to voice the
banal and familiar and a struggle to redefine the cliché in
terms of a more intimately pressing, if less violent, encounter
between man and woman. Significantly, in the last stanza,
the syntax also disintegrates under the pressure; the metrical
discontinuity of the first three stanzas invades the vocabulary
of the poem, and we're left with the insoluble ambiguities of
'vantage' and 'by'.

I think it's fair to say that the 'modernity' of all these poems
comes basically from the way that they tacitly recognize, with
Eliot, that the death has occurred of 'the language of poetry'.
From now on the poem has to do commerce with the many
languages of a linguistically pluralist society, of which
'poetic language' is only one. The poem itself has become a
mode, partly technical, partly ideological, of *experiencing*
language. And this has meant that the disinterestedness of
poetry, which it has inherited from the tradition, has been
carried into contemporary verse with a kind of partisan
fervour. Flicking one's way through any anthology of
recent poems, one senses a new spirit of linguistic imperial-

ism; each poet is out to stake a claim on the language it uses, to advertise its possession of a particular idiom. I suppose that the two most characteristic, and superficially divergent, lines from the verse written in the 1950s must be Larkin's 'Hatless I take off my cycle clips/ In awkward reverence' (from 'Church Going') and the opening of Ginsberg's beat-litany, 'Howl', 'I saw the best minds of my generation destroyed by madness, starving hysterical naked . . .' Yet, in an important way, these two lines do have a startling resemblence; both bring the language they use to a point of parody, making a preemptive bid to seize it for their particular poem. Larkin's clerical, down-at-heel, suburban voice and Ginsberg's beaded and belled version of Blake in his *Prophetic Books* represent two allied attempts to achieve authority for a single social tone. Both, I think, show signs of an instinctive realization that the poem now has to go out and fight in the street for the possession of its language; both recognize that there is no longer any culturally central idiom to provide a poetic Esperanto.

One ought, perhaps, to throw in a counter-example here. It's true that many poems now being published, both in England and the United States, seem to be written as if nothing much had changed since, say, the time when Tennyson was retiring to his study after breakfast to get on with the *Idylls*. While I was working on this chapter (November 1970) a freak cyclone brought devastating floods to the delta region of East Pakistan, killing around a quarter of a million people. Two weeks later a poem titled 'Empty Skies' appeared in *Tribune*, the British Socialist weekly:

> Suddenly nothing.
> The cyclone had burst into cosmic spittle
> and Mother Ganges swallowed her mantras.
> Blue squirted joyously across the sky,
> stillness slept on the fragile paddy-fields.
> Suddenly nothing.

The living picked their way, silently,
among the sodden dead, looking ahead.
Stillness was imaged at their feet,
shrugged overhead like a kite.
Water was foul and food fetid.
No bird flew out of the sun;
beyond the glutted waves they
swooped in vigil, clawed in combat.
From the silent water
damp smoke and heavy breathing rose
but were for days unanswered.
In the air nothing;
birds swooped and clawed elsewhere.

DAVID TRIBE

This is a very recognizable sort of poem. One can find dozens
like it in student magazines, and, indeed, in all those periodicals which publish contemporary (and often very amateur)
verse. It tries to work up immediate (and emotionally highly
charged) situations into the immortality thought to be
bestowed by 'poetry' and the stylized, vivid language that
goes with it. Yet its unselfconsciousness betrays it; the 'vivid-
ness' comes across as arch, the metaphors seem dead—not
because they are, in any literal sense, 'clichés', but because
that kind of verbal invention is fatally linked with a set of
literary conventions which we find antiquarian. The tone of
'Empty Skies' now belongs, indisputably, more to the personalized, on-the-spot TV report than to poetry. The kind of
society of likeminded-people-with-their-hearts-in-the-right-
places which it tacitly creates in the language it uses is a
society which has passed from the hands of Tennyson to the
hands of David Frost. The society of the poem today is more
self-conscious, more defensive, more knowing, more exclusive; it corresponds very much more exactly to the pluralist
tone and structure of the society we actually inhabit.

2

The Society of the Poem

A society which was like a really good poem, embodying
the aesthetic virtues of beauty, order, economy and
subordination of detail to the whole, would be a nightmare
of horror for, given the historical reality of actual men,
such a society could only come into being through selective
breeding, extermination of the physically and mentally unfit,
absolute obedience to its Director, and a large slave class
kept out of sight in cellars.

Vice versa, a poem which was really like a political
democracy—examples, unfortunately, exist—would be
formless, windy, banal and utterly boring.

W. H. AUDEN, 'The Poet and the City',
from *The Dyer's Hand*

One piece of linguistic whimsy which has passed, from sheer
embarrassment, from normal current usage is that Miss
Brodieish phrase 'the world of art', 'the world of poetry'.
Aside from its histrionic, indulgently Edwardian overtones,
the phrase's death was largely brought on by our belief, with
F. R. Leavis, that poems and other works of art properly
belong to the real, muddled world of ordinary human activity,
and do not constitute some aëry-faëry 'world of their own'.
Yet, in an important way, the expression does correspond to
a reality in our experience of reading verse. No-one, presum-
ably, climbed down into his air-raid shelter after reading
Peter Porter's 'Your Attention Please' in the last chapter.
(Although, when the poem was first broadcast on the B.B.C.
Third Programme, an American serviceman did ring up the
Corporation, asking whether an All Clear was likely to be
sounded.) If we grant that the language of the poem is the
language of society at large, that it is subject to the same

pressures and norms, limited in the same way by the historical process and by shared social experience, we shall also have to acknowledge that the poem is in the habit of taking some diabolical liberties with the medium to which it, like the individual human being in a society, owes its existence.

Such offensively elementary tit-bits of aesthetic theory have to be unpacked from the cupboard at this stage, if we are to consider the tantalizing metaphor (or, perhaps, a more-than-metaphor) that the poem, as a chunk of human language at its most ordered and contained, is a social structure, whose internal operations, contradictions, leaps in logic, and imaginative flights correspond at all points to latent features and movements in the society which surrounds it. We have now, I think, a stronger theoretical basis than ever before from which to examine this proposition. Those anthropologists who, like Claude Lévi Strauss, treat linguistics as the fundamental social science, and for whom all cultural activities, from cooking to religious ritual, find their source in the structure of the language in which they occur, have fortuitously bolstered literary criticism. Criticism, for all its faults, has at least developed a style for investigating language in a way that is uniquely sensitive to social and emotional tone, to the slightest aberrant twist of syntax, and to breaks in the consistency of a particular register. The French 'semiologist' Roland Barthes, himself a pupil and associate of Lévi Strauss, has already gone some way towards broking a marriage between criticism and anthropology in *Writing Degree Zero* (London, 1967). At the Birmingham University Centre for Contemporary Cultural Studies the relationship has been fostered, and has taken on the air of a long, and unconsummated, engagement. But generally this area of inquiry is more thick in hints and rumours than in tangible results. 'The sociology of literature' still tends to mean, alas, the sociology of almost everything—the writer, the literary 'background', the kind of society described by the novel or poem—except the work itself.

Yet the vocabulary of criticism, however loosely and un-consciously, has always treated literature in social terms. It groups particular works in hierarchies and 'traditions' which are expressions of a social structure just as much as they are 'pure' aesthetic valuations. (See Chapter 5.) It talked until recently of 'the world of the poem', crediting that world with a linguistic solidity which suggests that the reader can inhabit the literary work in a way parallel to his life in society outside. And, discussing the actual texture of verse, the main weapon in the critical armoury is still, however disguised, the hier-archy of styles ranging from 'high' to 'low' which has been directly transplanted from our experience as members of a complexly layered social system. There has, however, been a strong current of disapproval amongst both writers and critics against allowing these tacit metaphors full play. In the conservative ideology I discussed in the last chapter, repre-sented centrally by Eliot and the New Critics, 'society' and the poem are polarized—forced into opposition by the belief that they make up a kind of Manichean totality, with the forces of darkness locked in contest against the forces of light. The basic New Critical doctrine of the 'autonomy' of the poem (graven on the tablets in the 1940s by Wimsatt and Beardsley in their essays 'The Intentional Fallacy' and 'The Affective Fallacy') celebrated a Feast of Poetic Ascension in which the literary work, freed of all visible earthly chains, was seen to float miraculously into some Platonic super-sphere. Its return is now much overdue.

How, then, to map out the social geography of a poem? Does poetic order correspond in any detailed way to social order? What sort of regime is maintained in a particular verse structure, and does one enter it as a tourist or as a tax-paying citizen? Is the poet, as Auden suggests, inevitably cast in the role of dictator? I want to look closely at two quotations here, to try to test the society/poem metaphor; though one should keep in mind the fact that this kind of procedure is shaky at best, since it tends to feed into the poem the informa-

tion that one is claiming to get out of it. The first example is
a complete poem by Philip Larkin, 'Mr Bleaney':

'This was Mr Bleaney's room. He stayed
The whole time he was at the Bodies, till
They moved him.' Flowered curtains, thin and frayed,
Fall to within five inches of the sill,

Whose window shows a strip of building land,
Tussocky, littered. 'Mr Bleaney took
My bit of garden properly in hand.'
Bed, upright chair, sixty-watt bulb, no hook

Behind the door, no room for books or bags—
'I'll take it.' So it happens that I lie
Where Mr Bleaney lay, and stub my fags
On the same saucer-souvenir, and try

Stuffing my ears with cotton-wool, to drown
The jabbering set he egged her on to buy.
I know his habits—what time he came down,
His preference for sauce to gravy, why

He kept on plugging at the four aways—
Likewise their yearly frame: the Frinton folk
Who put him up for summer holidays,
And Christmas at his sister's house in Stoke.

But if he stood and watched the frigid wind
Tousling the clouds, lay on the fusty bed
Telling himself that this was home, and grinned
And shivered, without shaking off the dread

That how we live measures our own nature,
And at his age having no more to show
Than one hired box should make him pretty sure
He warranted no better, I don't know.

If one reads this aloud, one notices, I think, that there is some
sort of tussle going on between the social dimension of the
verse and the verbal patterns into which it is arranged. One
instantly senses the firm, underlying grip of the iambic

pentameter, the classical, elegiac rhythm of traditional English verse; and this metrical outline is strongly reinforced by the steady recurrence of those tinkling, monosyllabic rhymes. But neither the landlady nor the narrator of the poem seems altogether at home in the form. Indeed, the opening two words of the poem make up, not an iambic, but a trochaic foot, and there's another jarring reversed foot in the last line of the first stanza, 'Fall to'. In the second line the landlady's prattling voice runs clean away from the shape of the pentameter, in a flurry of unaccented syllables: 'Thĕ whóle tiṁe hĕ wǎs ǎt thĕ Bódiĕs'. From the moment it opens the poem gets entangled in the cross-fire between speech patterns and verse patterns, as if Larkin were falling over backwards to be fair to the irregular rhythms of both the voices in the dialogue. But this impression of fairness is belied by the way in which he enforces his line-endings. Each line is chopped off to suit the length of the pentameter, irrespective of the sense or syntax of its speaker. The result is a chronic case of compulsive enjambment, in which the language of the first five stanzas of the poem gets frequently treated as if it were so much faded ribbon, purchasable by the yard.

And this, in an important sense, is exactly what it is. The two voices in the poem are—in British terms—immediately recognizable as class spokesmen. The tired gentility of the narrator, with his waspish susceptibility to the annoyingly intrusive details of lower-class life, is loaded with Prufrockian ennui, with the kind of condescending irony that Wells lavished on poor Mr Polly. The landlady is there, like every Mrs Mop in the history of English fiction, to interrupt, to utter spine-chilling clichés in a voice as stale and predictable as cheap scent. Both characters are sprinkled by Larkin with a layer of fine grey dust. When the narrator begins, like an exhausted novelist, to reinvent Mr Bleaney and his 'habits' he does so by producing catalogues like grocers' lists, larded with strained impersonations of the sort of vaguely racy slang Mr Bleaney himself might be imagined to employ: 'stub my

fags . . . why/He kept on plugging at the four aways'. Yet
they are both sustained by the steady, returning swing of the
base-rhythm of the poem; it lends them a kind of dignity and
seriousness that one feels they should, by rights, have
forfeited.

It's not until the beginning of the sixth stanza that the poem
abruptly achieves consonance. From the phrase 'But if', which
works in this context almost like a rhetorical invocation, the
iambic beat slows and becomes more regular; the vocabulary
thickens, becomes richly figurative; the line-endings start to
coincide with syntactical pauses; the entire tone becomes more
assured, more resonant. We have moved from a grubby,
Wellsian—and Orwellian—version of lower-middle-class life
which won't fit into verse to nothing less than the hallowed
and formal language of poetry. As Larkin gets into his stride
in the last, breathlessly long sentence he retrieves an extraordinarily clean and austere metaphor from the welter of
shabby details which went to compose the first five stanzas.
But it is a seedy and incomplete victory of poetic order over
the uncontained and shapeless society with which the poem
began. In the last line and a half the rhetorical confidence
drains away into a shrug; it's hard, in fact, reading the final
stanza aloud, to deliver the 'I don't know' in any tone other
than a petulant mutter. Yet the phrase is grammatically
dependent on a series of much earlier syntactical manoeuvres:
'But if he . . . without . . .' In other words, the shrug is
anticipated, built in, even at the poem's highest point of
rhetorical richness and assurance.

'Mr Bleaney' does actually strike me, *pace* Auden, as a
remarkably successful example of a poem which is very much
like a political democracy of a peculiarly muddled and English
kind. It is multilingual, and each idiom corresponds exactly
to a social tone, even if the idioms are defined in rather literary
terms: the declassed 'narrator', the proletarian 'character',
and the essentially aristocratic voice of 'poetry'. But the
transactions which take place within this simple structure

are subtle and complicated; they entail a constant bargaining between the order imposed by the institution of the poem and the separate kinds of life which go on within each individual language. If an authoritative voice does finally emerge it is a voice which has won its honesty of tone by a process of hard compromise; and, indeed, honesty has become a matter of being able to bypass all the rhetorical alternatives offered by the poem with a bleakly direct negative. We are asked to respect and like, not the utterance itself, so much as the process of compromise which has gone into its making. I think if one were looking for a working definition of the tone of English liberalism one couldn't find a better example than 'Mr Bleaney'. One may resent its air of resigned righteousness, but one can't miss the richness with which it invests its linguistic community in the search for a voice—however minimal—that will cut across the barriers of class and rhetoric and speak direct.

My second example is the first two stanzas of 'Bubbs Creek Haircut' by Gary Snyder:

High ceiling'd and the double mirrors, the
     calendar a splendid alpine scene—scab barber—
in stained white barber gown, alone, sat down, old man
A summer fog gray San Francisco day
I walked right in. on Howard street
               haircut a dollar twenty-five.
Just clip it close as it will go.
    'now why you want your hair cut back like that.'
    —well I : m going to the Sierras for a while
Bubbs Creek and on across to upper Kern.
          he wriggled clippers,
'Well I been up there, I built the cabin
    up at Cedar Grove. In nineteen five.'
       old haircut smell

Next door, Goodwill.
                              where I came out.
A search for sweater, and a stroll
                              in the board & concrete room of
                    unfixed junk downstair—
All emblems of the past—too close—
            heaped up in chilly dust and bare bulb glare
Of tables, wheelchairs, battered trunks & wheels
& pots that boiled up coffee nineteen ten, *things*
Swimming on their own & finally freed
                                   from human need. Or?
            waiting a final flicker of desire
To tote them out once more. Some freakish use.
The Master of the limbo drag-leggd watches
                                   making prices
        to the people seldom buy
The sag-asst rocker has to make it now. Alone.

Where Larkin was busy exploiting the dissonances between
his speakers and the verse shape of the poem, Snyder rolls
them all into a kind of harmonious community. 'Bubbs Creek
Haircut' has a similar structure of ghostly iambs to give the
verse its rhythmic momentum. But where in 'Mr Bleaney' the
reversed feet and doubled stresses were deliberately played
against the imposed pattern of the poem, here they are syncopated; incorporated into a lazy, lolloping rhythm that swings
right the way through each stanza. The voices of the narrator
and the barber blend in a pattern of continuous stresses, as if
they were playing parts in a musical duo:

        Just clip it close as it will go.
                'now why you want your hair cut back like that.'

People, place names, narrative, and the lumber of physical
objects are all accommodated within this easy rhythmical
scheme. The world of the poem—quite unlike American
society outside it—has a homogeneous, organic life of its own,
controlled by a voice which, poles apart from Larkin's
splintered and localized idioms, seems capable of saying
anything. It can even talk in an explicitly 'poetic' way without

disturbing the evenness of its flow. In the lines

> Swimming on their own & finally freed
> > from human need. Or?
> waiting a final flicker of desire
> To tote them out once more.

we get phrases that might have been lifted from Eliot's *Four Quartets* sitting side by side with Snyder's casual, hitch-hiker's diction. 'Bubbs Creek Haircut' stolidly refuses to play along with the theory of the dissociation of sensibility; it creates the basic vocabulary and grammar of a language in which haircuts and metaphysics, history and junk, can be articulated by a single voice.

But Snyder's voice is not, in any immediately recognizable way, a legatee of 'poetic language'. The poem provides a special area in which styles which are normally mutually exclusive can be reconciled; it is a utopian structure. But its utopia corresponds to the ideals of a specific social group: the new hobos with their Zen and their macrobiotic foods and their basic mistrust of rationalist categories. Snyder's poem works in a cool, universalist rhetoric which blurs all distinctions between people and things, and treats ideas as if they were animate objects: it is an attempt to create a total discourse, a fully organic and articulated society. The verse itself functions like a commune, and has the same flavour of neo-pastoral. In 1959, in response to Donald M. Allen's request for a statement on poetics (included in Allen's *The New American Poetry*), Snyder wrote:

> I've just recently come to realize that the rhythms
> of my poems follow the rhythm of the physical work
> I'm doing and life I'm leading at any given time—
> which makes the music in my head which creates the
> line. Conditioned by the poetic tradition of the
> English language & whatever feeling I have for the
> sound of poems I dig in other languages . . .

But 'work' for Snyder turns out to mean a pretty limited range of activities: laying cobblestones on mountain roads (the source of his collection, *Riprap*), working on timber plantations, hitch-hiking across the U.S.A., or, as in 'Bubbs Creek Haircut', barbering—occupations which have the individual and varied rhythm of a craft. Aside from the peculiar magic of the long-distance truck, industrialization is completely excluded from the society of Snyder's verse. In fact, his poems have a reassuringly familiar air (interestingly, he is the only young West Coast poet who has received any hospitality from the *Critical Quarterly*), like William Morris craft-factories transplanted to the alien terrain of California.

There is, though, one important difference between the ways in which Larkin's and Snyder's poems work. It is impossible, I think, to read 'Mr Bleaney' with much sympathy unless one is prepared to enter it as an inhabitant; to undergo the shifts and strains which it imposes upon the reader as the victim of its mixed and uneasy society. We have, for the time being, to believe that it is written in the only language available both to it and to us. Characteristically of the English liberal style, the very sensibleness of its tone makes a bid for absolute social centrality; alternatives and resolutions beyond the reach of the narrow and ordinary voice at its centre must strike us, at the outset, as likely to be eccentric or silly. This tacit appeal to common sense assumes a much wider complicity between the writer and his readers; we're expected to share the same assumptions, the same grumbles, the same prejudices, the same gloomy resignation to the exhaustion of possibilities. To enter the poem is to wear a patched Harris tweed jacket, to earn £950 per year, to vote, with certain reservations, for the Labour Party at General Elections, and to ride a bicycle.

Snyder's poem, by contrast, hardly makes hitch-hikers of us all. We are allowed to attend 'Bubbs Creek Haircut' as spectators, for the latent tensions and dissonances of its language have been resolved before we arrive. All the poem needs is our approval or recognition. Its utopian structure

gives it a completeness and a quality of schematization that
make it more a demonstration of form than an involving web
in which the reader is caught, and, as in Larkin's poem, has to
fight to get out. But, of course, it is true that both these poems
do, in the broadest sense of the word, 'mimic' an idiom which
we can quickly identify as belonging to a particular social
area; Hull-seedy and California-bejeaned. What about those
poems which seem to deliberately attempt to sever their
language from a recognizable social context? What kind, if
any, of social community is created by verse which roots
itself firmly in mythological, or ritual, or rhetorical sources,
and which actively tries to transcend the particularities of a
society at a single place and time?

For a large number of young writers (now more a critical
term than a description of age, since Allen Ginsberg is
currently pushing fifty) in both Britain and the U.S.A. Blake's
Prophetic Books have provided an escape-chute from the
here-and-now of a society that they are dedicated to rejecting.
They have adopted the mantles of Bards, Prophets, and Priests;
turned to the East for their religion; gone to the no-man's land
of the Past for their language.

> Allen Ginsberg says this: I am
>   a mass of sores and worms
>   & baldness & belly & smell
>   I am false Name the prey
>   of Yamantaka Devourer of
>   Strange dreams, the prey of
>   radiation & Police Hells of Law
>
> I am that I am I am the
>   man & the Adam of hair in
>   my loins. This is my spirit and
>   physical shape I inhabit
>   this Universe Oh weeping
>   against what is my
>   own nature for now

This is a style which, by its promiscuous archaism, tries to dissolve time and history into a kind of cosmic community of like minds. Ginsberg, Blake, the Zen Masters, and selected characters from the Old Testament, all sit about, like so many survivors of a balloon debate, floating in the pure stratosphere of poetic space. Only a rudimentary syntax still exists, and the characteristic grammatical gesture is the & sign, along with the repetitious formulae of the litany (like the word 'who', which begins almost every line in Part 1 of 'Howl')— devices for springing the most unlikely conjunctions on the reader as if they were the most natural connections in the world. The 'physical shape' and the universe which Ginsberg inhabits, weeping against his own nature, has, not surprisingly, become wholly alienated from the 'spirit', with its astronautical capacities for breaking the time-barrier. Indeed, space travel has become a central metaphor for the New Blakeans, promising an ultimate, electronic correlative to the dizzying Apollo programmes of their syntax and vocabulary. If a society can be said to exist in their verse it is an even bigger village than any dreamed up by Marshall McLuhan; a-temporal, trans-global, para-mythological. Its most confident celebrant to date has been, a little oddly, perhaps, the British poet Edwin Morgan, who wrote a sort of lusty school song on the occasion of the Albert Hall 'Poetry International' event in June 1965:

> Worldscene! Worldtime! Spacebreaker! Wildship! Starman!
> Gemini man dangles white and golden—the world floats
> on a gold cord and curves blue white beautiful below him—
> Vostok shrieks and prophesies, Mariner's prongs flash—
> to the wailing of Voskhod Earth sighs, she shakes men loose
>   at last—
> out, in our time, to be living seeds sent far beyond
> even imagination, though imagination is awake—take
> poets on your voyages! Prometheus
> embraces Icarus and in a gold shell with wings
> he launches him up through the ghostly detritus

of gods and dirty empires and dying laws,
he mounts, he cries, he shouts, he shines, he streams
like new light done, his home is in a sun
and he shall be the burning unburned one.
In darkness, Daedalus
embraces Orpheus . . .

But even Morgan allows a frankly realistic note to enter his verse in the plaintiveness of the appeal, 'take/ poets on your voyages!'; and so far the Apollo missions have been more remarkable for their technological accomplishments than for their rather unhappy ventures into the arts of language. Much more than Snyder these poets are openly utopian in the structure and idiom they use in their verse. Ginsberg and Michael McClure in the United States, Michael Horovitz and his peripatetic cronies in Britain, and the lyrics of the Doors in pop music have aspired to use language as if the surrounding society were merely a 'ghostly detritus/ of gods and dirty empires and dying laws'. And, of course, one of the central functions of the 'counter culture' is to operate as if the revolution had already arrived. Prophecy is at its most successful when it switches from the future to the present tense. On both sides of the Atlantic the Underground has its own communication system, its own rules of kinship and marriage, its own institutions. Within the subculture for which the *International Times* is the parish magazine, gatherings like the Albert Hall 'Poetry International' and pronouncements from the temple astrologers that the Age of Aquarius is upon us have the status of world events of unquestionable authority. All this has enabled the existence of a language which looks as weird to the outsider as it seems conventional to the inhabitant of the parish. The Underground, in fact, presents an extreme and diagrammatic model of what is happening continuously in other areas of contemporary verse; and I want to return to this question in later chapters, to explore the way in which the idioms of particular social groups claim poetic authority and centrality. Writers working from within universities, or publishing their poetry in magazines with a notable poetic ideology, like Ian Hamilton's *The Review* (or, in an only slightly less marked way, *Partisan Review* in the U.S.), or speaking for a single region or class, tend to display similar utopian characteristics in their attempt to give their language the completeness of a whole and habitable society.

There do seem to me to be a number of important exceptions to my general argument; poems whose language makes society conspicuous by its absence, which work in an idiom that has been refined—or mutilated—to exclude the kinds of relationship and resonance one expects of a full, functioning social vernacular. Over the last few years Ted Hughes has been working on a series of poems, some of which have been published in his collection *Crow*, written in a style which is neither socially mimetic nor utopian. He appears, in fact, to have reinvented a language for himself, drawn partly from folk-tales, partly from the rhythms and vocabulary of Yorkshire dialect, partly from mythology and epic literature, which has the cold, unsocial force of stone. Crow, the central figure and voice of the series, is the kind of super-bird one might encounter in a horror comic written by John Milton: black, primeval, Adamic; whose power is vested somewhere between the sharpness of his talons and the cosmic irony of his laughter; whose entire being is concentrated into the terrifying, solipsistic art of sheer survival. Crow has gone beyond society, beyond language:

> Crow whistled.
> Words attacked him with the glottal bomb—
> He wasn't listening.
> Words surrounded and over-ran him with light aspirates—
> He was dozing.
> Words infiltrated guerrilla labials—
> Crow clapped his beak, scratched it.
> Words swamped him with consonantal masses—
> Crow took a sip of water and thanked heaven.

Words retreated, suddenly afraid
Into the skull of a dead jester
Taking the whole world with them—

But the world did not notice.

And Crow yawned—long ago
He had picked that skull empty.

This is written in a kind of calculated doggerel. It has the repetitions and the violent hyperboles of the nastier sort of Germanic fairy-story; each line is isolated in space, syntactically complete; its metaphors are large and elemental, drawn equally from the vocabularies of war and folk mythology. The complete absence of grammatical qualifications and leisured linkages gives the language the air of a poetic telegraphese; it feels like an abnormal communication. It excludes society like a nightmare, or a psychosis. When Crow speaks he talks in an idiom so drastically reduced that it takes the form of a foreboding, whitened skull of language, a skeletal *memento mori*. Here is the central section of 'Crow's Account of the Battle':

The cartridges were banging off, as planned,
The fingers were keeping things going
According to excitement and orders.
The unhurt eyes were full of deadliness.
The bullets pursued their courses
Through clods of stone, earth and skin,
Through intestines, pocket-books, brains, hair, teeth
According to Universal Laws.
And mouths cried 'Mamma'
From sudden traps of calculus,
Theorems wrenched men in two,
Shock-severed eyes watched blood
Squandering as from a drain-pipe
Into the blanks between stars.
Faces slammed down into clay
As for the making of a life-mask.

Knew that even on the sun's surface
They could not be learning more or more to the point.
Reality was giving its lesson,
Its mishmash of scripture and physics,
With here, brains in hands, for example,
And there, legs in a treetop.
There was no escape except into death.
And still it went on—it outlasted
Many prayers, many a proved watch,
Many bodies in excellent trim,
Till the explosives ran out
And sheer weariness supervened
And what was left looked round at what was left.

One can't fail to notice that Crow's narrative is crammed full of the most ordinary clichés drawn from war movies and war memoirs; it's a patchwork quilt of quite familiar bits of language. What is so disconcerting is that they happen here in a completely disordered way, and have got alarmingly mixed up with all sorts of worryingly specific *things*, like 'intestines, pocket-books, brains, hair, teeth'. The normal functions of grammar and tone—to keep one category apart from another, to relate separate components in a rational sequence—have been bypassed. Society has failed to impose its customary order upon experience. We are left with Crow-doggerel, the bloodied stumps of language that remain after things have fallen apart.

3
The Cat's-Cradle

Will that cat's-cradle hold our baby?
I mean, for instance, this Byronic
Writing keeps architectonic
Principles entirely other
Than those so sadly missed by Mother;
Woefully linear, not to say
Rambling. Now, is this a way
To write, from now on quite uncouth,
Not qualified to tell the truth?
                    DONALD DAVIE, 'First Epistle to Eva Hesse'

The doctrine of imitative form has been ferociously pursued by the American critic Yvor Winters as a 'fallacy'. But it is a fallacy that has haunted the shape and texture of contemporary verse. Much of the energy of the modernist movement has been concentrated into the search for congruency between the style of the poem and the ways in which language is felt to function in the world outside. The cheery prophets of the linguistic millennium—McLuhan, Marcuse, Susan Sontag —have, a bit prematurely, danced all over the coffin of language, condemning us to a world without rhythm or syntax, where the engulfing silence is only broken by the occasional obscenity or ejaculation of despair. World-order, so they say, has ceased to correspond with word-order: we live on the dangerous edge of ungrammaticalness, trapeze artists of the abyss, supported on a frail skein of language that is dissolving under our feet. It sounds a bad time for poets. If verse is language at its most fully organized and arranged, can its elaborate syntactical structures, its recurrent metrical patterns, its reflexive contingencies of rhyme, work as anything other than ironic reminders of an ordered universe that went absent without leave somewhere around the year 1917?

'It came to me,' remarked William Carlos Williams in *I Wanted to Write a Poem*, 'that the concept of the foot itself would have to be altered in our new relativistic world.' And, more than any other poem of its period, Williams's rag-bag city epic *Paterson* came close to matching the cat's-cradle of its linguistic patterns to the deformed and squawking baby of language as it is used in the heterogeneous context of a modern urban environment. *Paterson* is a collage poem; it treats language, like one of Marcel Duchamps's 'ready-mades', as something *found*. Williams's snippets of history and gossip and conversation, his fragments of classical literary modes juxtaposed against modern American vernacular, are orchestrated rather than created. The force of the poem comes not from its capacity to invent so much as from its ability to assimilate all the bits and pieces of language that happen to lie around it. Reading *Paterson* is like living in a city between the covers of a book; strangers live their separate lives, headlines assume sudden meaning, literary fragments rise to the surface and as quickly disappear, odd words and phrases become momentarily audible. Every venture into speech is a breaking of the silence which surrounds the poem.

Williams's notion of the 'variable foot' allowed him to introduce chance and silence as active presences in his verse. For the fixed foot—the di-DAH di-DAH di-DAH of syllable-counted metrics—sets up a static design for the poem, against which every successive verbal performance has to be measured; each line works as a fulfilment or a rejection of the prediction made by the shape of the first line of the poem. To take the boringly classic instance, Gray's *Elegy*, where

The *Curfew* tolls the Knell of parting Day

falls, as exactly as any chunk of language can, into the schoolbook grid of alternating stresses: ˇ —/ˇ —/ˇ —/ˇ —/ˇ —. A perfectly phrased iambic pentameter. It also works as a prophecy, giving us a speech pattern into which we try to fit

every utterance in the poem. But fifty lines on there comes a
word-sequence which jars a little against the smooth iambic
mould:

> Rich with the Spoils of Time did ne'er unroll;
> Chill Penury repress'd their noble Rage,
> And froze the genial Current of the Soul.

One has to give a fairly strong stress to the word 'Rich' in
order to make grammatical sense of the first line, and this
tends to island and accentuate the word, since it brings one
into conflict with the basic verse pattern. With 'Chill Penury'
the iambic pentameter is further disturbed: the pattern calls
for 'chill PEN/ u RY', while sense demands 'CHILL PENury'.
But order is formally restored in the final line, with a return
to the even rhythm established at the beginning of the poem.
A fixed-foot metre of this sort provides a guarantee that the
verse will be a continuous body of language. The recurrence
of the rhythm prevents the words from disappearing into a
void of silence. Individual lines and words may nudge and
jostle against the predictive pattern of the metre, but they
can never normally destroy it. It's a confident form, promising
a style secure from the invasions of irregular time and from
the hunger of an engulfing silence at the edge of the poem.
Williams needed to get rid of the predictions and the guarantees of regular metre. Each line becomes a new happening;
potentially, at least, it is unaffected by the shape of what has
gone before. Silence can enter the verse at any point, and the
language of the poem is subjected to the constant play of
the random upon its texture. Williams follows the chancy
rhythms of ordinary American speech, embracing the spoken
word in its contingent imposition upon silence as a structural
correlative to 'our new relativistic world'. Here, from Book
4 of *Paterson*, is a characteristic dialogue:

> —on the couch, kissing and talking while his
> hands explored her body, slowly   .
> courteously   .   persistent   .

Be careful
I've got an awful cold

It's the first
this year. We went
fishing in all
that rain last week

Who? Your father?
—and my boy friend

Fly fishing?
No. Bass. But it isn't

the season. I know that
but nobody saw us

I got soaked to the skin
Can you fish?

Oh I have a pole and a
line and just fish along

We caught quite a few

.   .   .   .

We hear the conversation as a single linguistic event; the two
voices are orchestrated and rhythmically organized so that
they form a kind of syncopated cadenza. There's no metrical
or logical continuity, so that the dialogue exists, tensely, on
the verge of obliteration. Every line is a new beginning, a
sally into the surrounding silence. And that silence is visually
marked on the page by spaces and full stops; the large, un-
populated area of the poem. The effect of this sequence is like
listening to silence made real in a theatre by introducing some
minimal noise—a twitter of birdsong or the sound of rain
falling. At a level of more self-conscious artistic activity one
could compare it with John Cage's experiments, both musical
and linguistic, with the aural and temporal texture of silence.

We are made aware of the possibility—and the small, furtive, irregular triumphs—of language and sound by being brought face to face with the silence from which all words must grow.

Williams has had a huge effect on recent American poetry; the techniques he explored in *Paterson* have been subsequently canonized, to form a one-man counter-tradition to trade against the collected works of Eliot, Wallace Stevens, and the East Coast-and-campus aristos of contemporary verse. Williams's gospel of silence and the variable foot, and his implicit doctrine that the form a poem takes must imitate the discontinuity, the contingency, the disjunctive social patterns of life in an industrial society, was preached from the tabernacle of Black Mountain College in the late 1940s and through the 1950s. The late Charles Olson was rector of Black Mountain, and, like a latter-day Pound, gathered round him an impressive group of apostles, including Robert Creeley, Robert Duncan, Ed Dorn, John Wieners, and Jonathan Williams. In a series of blasts and essays the Black Mountaineers constructed a sort of charter of liberation for poetic form. The fixed foot was to give way to the line, as measured by the breath of the speaker; logical syntax was to be replaced by the vocal activity of a dynamic grammar; the poem was to turn into a happening 'as of the thingitself', lifted off the page and into the space-time continuum. The entire enterprise was christened by Olson 'Projective Verse'. The sole anchor by which the poem was prevented from floating off altogether into the inter-stellar spaces was, in Olson's word, *topos*—the place where it happened, and from which it drew its particular language.

As a theory of poetics Projectivism has the appealing literal-mindedness of medieval theology. It carries mimetic realism as the sole touchstone of formal structure to a point of mystical absurdity. One might, for instance, be struck by the curious verbal feel of these lines from Olson's *Maximus Poems:*

But that which matters, that which insists, that which will last
where shall you find it, my people, where shall you listen
when all is become billboards, when all, even silence, is
when even the gulls,
my roofs,
when even you, when sound itself

It sounds a little like a nineteenth-century political harangue which has lost some of its key words, like a page with a tear running down one edge. But its oddity has a much more impressive explanation. Writing in the *Black Mountain Review* in 1956, Robert Duncan provided some general 'Notes on poetics regarding Olson's maximus':

> that the breath-blood circulation be gaind, an *interjection*! the levels of the passions and inspirations in *phrases*; second, that focus be gaind, a *substantive*, the level of vision; and third, the complex of muscular gains that are included in taking hold and balancing, *verbs*, but more, the *movement of the language*, the *level* of the ear, the hand, and the foot. All these incorporated in *measure*.

Robert Creeley, quoting this passage in 1958, adds in a footnote: 'Duncan has given, *in fine*, the steps of a poetic *grammar*'. So the word *is*, dangling at the end of the third line of my Olson quotation, is really a complex of muscular gains that are included in taking hold and balancing; the long sequence of relative phrases at the beginning make up a balanced series of levels of passion and inspiration; the people, billboards, silence, gulls, roofs, and sound are points of focus, levels of vision, and so on. The trouble is that, whether flat on the page or live in space and time, this section of the poem needs to be transliterated into Duncan's terms before it becomes articulate. The new freedom begins to look startlingly like a very old kind of rhetorical pedantry. Indeed, the Projectivists' relentless attention to such real or imagined psycho-dynamics of language resembles nothing so much as the ill-fated enterprise of Funes the Memorious in Jorge Luis Borges' story: the attempt to construct a system of numeration in which every number was to have the name of a specific thing—8000, for instance, was known as 'The Railroad'. Funes died of pulmonary congestion. Language *is* language precisely because it is not a collection of things; speech, its physical dimension, is *communicative* noise because it is generated within a shared and recognized symbolic system. The Black Mountaineers, when they try to turn syntax into a series of physical events, simply offer us another symbolic system with which to decode the symbolic system we already have.

But, whatever the logical inconsistencies entailed in their programme, the Black Mountaineers have been a powerful ideological force in contemporary poetics. By treating the poem as an event—vulnerable, as all events are, to the haphazard buffeting of time and chance—and by using the words on the page as a kind of score for a spoken performance, they have brought the language and structure of verse very much closer to the conditions of speech. For the Black Mountaineers, as for Williams, the moment of articulation, of composition, is all; a man speaking carries the authenticity of history in his voice. It is in the play of language as happening that the poem occurs. In the words of Charles Olson, 'Is it not the PLAY of a mind we are after, is not that that shows whether a mind is there at all?' The main problem of Projective Verse lies, as with so much realist art, in the essential literalness of its approach to language; it is most successful as a formula when it is used to dramatize the consciousness of a half-wit whose mind is only capable of moving in a slow grammatical progression from one large, dumb object to another.

The point is that the Black Mountain 'cat's-cradle' is just as schematic in its own way as the traditional frame of metrics and syntax which it has tried to replace. Its bellicose rhetorical confidence (in part a product of its conservative assumptions about the instant availability of history and the organic nature of a certain kind of provincial life) belies its proclaimed doubts about the authority of language in a discontinuous world. It's no coincidence that when Olson gets into his stride he adopts the rolling tones of a mid-Victorian preacher, secure in his knowledge that he's a pillar of a society based on good epical rock. He makes the space-time continuum into an environment about as large, chilling, and empty as Cheltenham.

Imitative form, in its search for a poetic structure that will correspond to the fragmentariness, the unpredictability, and the unauthoritative texture of life outside the poem, has had a number of more worried, and, for me, more plausible, exponents. Significantly, those writers who have believed most fervently that the only kind of verse now possible is a verse stripped and degraded by the ravages of history, have tended to emerge from Central Europe. Experience of war, occupation, shifting political frontiers, and the incredible, nightmare inhumanity of fascist totalitarianism have thrown the niceties of language into more acute question than has been possible in Britain and the U.S.A. Tadeusz Rózewicz, a Pole, began his collection *Faces of Anxiety* with an aesthetic statement of black resignation:

MY POETRY

explains nothing
clarifies nothing
makes no sacrifices
does not embrace everything
does not redeem any hopes

. . . if it's not a fancy language
if it speaks without originality
if it holds no surprises
evidently this is how things ought to be.

His verse has been reduced to a language of flat statement and a grammar which is dominated by nouns—the names of the dreadful things which his poetry is forced to accommodate. Metaphors are almost entirely excluded; only the most ordinary adjectives are permitted; each poem is phrased in the blank rhythms of functional prose. (Comments on poems in

translation are always suspect, but Rózewicz makes his
linguistic intentions so clear, that in his case the features of
his style transcend the particularities of the Polish language.)
In 'Pigtail', dated 1948, in the Museum at Auschwitz,
Rózewicz writes:

> Behind clean glass
> the stiff hair lies
> of those suffocated in gas chambers
> there are pins and side combs
> in this hair
>
> . . . In huge chests
> clouds of dry hair
> of those suffocated
> and a faded plait
> a pigtail with a ribbon
> pulled at school
> by naughty boys.

No verse written in English has gone as far in this direction
of linguistic exhaustion as the work of Rózewicz and his
compatriot Zbigniew Herbert. Our language has not been
decimated by disasters of such appalling scope. English and
American poetry survives in an atmosphere thick with
rumours and intimations of impending chaos, but its essential
tone is one of fretful unease, of the broken slumber enjoyed,
perhaps, by the inhabitants of Auden's war-time city 'whose
terrible future may have just arrived'—in the person of a
sombre, clerkly figure stepping off a train with an attaché-
case. For us the clerk has not yet come; or, if he has, we are
unsure of his identity.

Interestingly, it is not among the more obvious millennial
groups, like the Underground and the West Coast writers, that
Anglo-American verse has taken a stricken form, but in the
work of a notorious aristo, inheritor of the New England
tradition, classical scholar, and urbane wit, Robert Lowell.
His most recent collection, *Notebook* (see also Chapter 9), is an

eloquent exploration of imitative form, in which metre, syntax, and rhyme are held at the point of total disintegration. *Notebook* is a sonnet-sequence—or, rather, a sequence of ruined sonnets. For, although every poem in the book is fourteen lines long, the rhyme-scheme has disappeared, except for occasional chance couplets, and the syntax has lost all trace of the mellifluous order and pretty shapes of the traditional sonnet. Lowell's idiom zigzags brokenly between the polarities of public and private life, between intense metaphor and plain statement, between polished aphorism and asyntactical nonsense. In the society of his poetry, language is seen to be on the edge of some terrible deterioration, about to topple over into the abyss of Chomsky's famous meaningless sentence, 'Sleep ideas furiously colourless green'. Lowell explores this idea in a line and situation of reverberating menace, in an anti-sonnet called 'The Restoration'. An exiled king returns to his study in the palace in the company of a policeman. Everything has changed; vandals have ripped the pictures out of their frames; his correspondence has been dealt with, his books desecrated. Then, Lowell writes:

> He halts at woman-things that can't be his
> He says, 'To think that human beings did this!'
> The sergeant picks up a defiled *White Goddess,* or is it
> *Secret Memoirs of the Courts of Europe*?
> 'Would a human beings do this things to these book?'

The figure of that policeman, and the violence he does to language—as to experience—haunts the collection. The breakdown of the syntax of the sentence becomes profoundly associated with the ungrammatical politics of the Chicago Democratic Convention in 1968, with order enforced at the end of a night-stick, or a rifle, or a gas canister. There is no syntax in a nightmare, and for, as he calls himself, 'A lapsed R.C. caught mid-journey to atheist' the grammar has dropped out of death. 'The Restoration' forces a naked confrontation to take place, between a civilized, but decadent, order and the brutal unlanguage of the new regime. The form of Lowell's 'sonnets' has been violated by the policemen who stalk inside them, twisting their sentences, breaking the backs of their rhythms, prolonging the line-ends and unhooking the rhymes. The crude assonance of the first couplet of my quotation—the link between 'his' and 'this'—is as near to poetry as a Chicago cop or a National Guardsman can come.

Imitative form entails an Aristotelian faith in the solidity of the external world, as well as in the doctrine that the poem is like any other social institution, say, a hospital, or a prison; dependent on the annual allocation of public funds, subject to the prevailing ideology of the government in power, and effective in direct proportion to its provision for a statistically ascertainable public need. Some poetic structures do seem to hold themselves directly answerable to a publicly recognizable version of sociographic structure; a discontinuous society is seen to demand a discontinuous verse, a broken hierarchy finds expression in broken syntax, the fragmented and pluralist use of language outside the poem turns, in verse, into a deliberate arhythmicality, into the planned sabotage of metre. But such rigid realism, with its deterministically literal laws of poetic cause and effect, is only one of a number of current literary ideologies. Its claims for primacy are part of the politics of poetry, and I shall return to them in the next chapter. Poems, to continue the institutional metaphor, have the heartening—and sometimes alarming—habit of refusing to be the sort of organizations likely to be subsidized by the government or local authority; like funhouses, brothels, and labyrinths, they frequently reflect the pressures of the society in which they occur only by their insistent subversiveness or libertarianism.

How, for instance, does one respond to the obsessive rhymes, the regular metre, and the incantatory grammar of some of Sylvia Plath's last poems?

You do not do, you do not do
Any more, black shoe
In which I have lived like a foot
For thirty years, poor and white,
Barely daring to breathe or Achoo.

Daddy, I have had to kill you.
You died before I had time—
Marble-heavy, a bag full of God,
Ghastly statue with one grey toe
Big as a Frisco seal

And a head in the freakish Atlantic
Where it pours bean green over blue
In the waters off beautiful Nauset.
I used to pray to recover you.
Ach, du.

'Daddy'

These stanzas come from a poem which has been widely celebrated for its treatment of, among other things, death, concentration camps, Electra complexes, and the plight of Jewishness. Under the inspection of a critic like A. Alvarez, 'Daddy' becomes a masterpiece of responsible psychological realism. But we shouldn't miss the fact that the poem is, before anything else, a game. It has rules (not unlike those of skipping rhymes), it exercises a euphoric freedom in its discovery of chance verbal resemblances (particularly in the 'You'/'Jew' rhyme and the sequence of 'two', 'blue', 'do', 'through' which it generates), and its recurrent flights into the primary-coloured vocabulary and images of the nursery help to ensure that it remains fancifully self-contained. The cat's cradle, instead of being changed to accommodate the baby, is used as a mode of changing the baby's nature. The style of the nursery rhyme transforms the Jews and Nazis of the poem into so many masked golliwogs; and the speaker addresses her father as a small girl might shake a rag doll. The poem only seems to me to be 'about' the conflicts it uses in the same way as

> Ring-a-ring o' roses,
> A pocket full of posies,
>   Atishoo! Atishoo!
> We all fall down.

is 'about' the Great Plague (whose symptoms provide the symbolized roses, posies, and sneezes of the nursery rhyme). The 'play' of the poem-as-game may, as here, be closer to the therapeutic fun offered by Plasticine and pieces of string in the schizoid ward of a mental hospital than it is to more disinterested forms of amusement, but we should not mistake it for realism. The poem, for Sylvia Plath, provides a liberated zone in which language can be played with, without fear of causing an explosion. The hard, external world of politics and psychosis enters her verse, not by force, but by invitation.

Rhyme, metre, and all the tricks and devices of imposed form offer the basic design and materials with which to construct an alternative, libidinous reality within the poem. Increasingly during the last ten years or so they have been used as signals; pointing up the change of dimension involved in crossing from the world outside to the world of verse; announcing our entrance to a pleasure dome where normal logic has dissolved into the rhyme and the pun, where the broken temporal sequences of everyday life have been drastically rearranged to compose the speeding repetitions and continuities of metre. In Ian Hamilton Finlay's collection *The Dancers Inherit the Party* (a title which neatly expresses precisely this notion of the poem as a triumphant game played in the debris of history) there is a poem called 'Catch':

> There once was a fisherman of Scrabster
> Caught in his pot a gey queer lapster.
>
> Thought he, this lapster's a sure sellar,
> A tail it has, and a wee propellor,
>
> In fact, its no ordinary lapster felly,
> It looks far more like a peedie heli-

You know yon kind of hoverlapster,
A what do you call it, helicapster.

Aye, aye, it's a peedie helicapster:
There's lots are caught in the sea off Scrabster.

The social pressures which feed nearly all Finlay's poems are
still just visible in 'Catch': the voices of crofters and fisher-
men, wary and defensive about the new technology invading
the patterns of their lives. The smugly offhand tone of the
last line is a wonderful reproduction of the style of the crafty
peasant, mixing knowingness and bewilderment in his hope-
ful assertion that there's nothing new under the sun. But the
jog-trot rhythm and the absurd rhymes turn the poem into a
brilliant, enclosed universe in which a language rich in puns,
malapropisms, and strange stories is given its head. The aural
and metrical qualities of the words themselves are allowed to
take over; drawing, from the jumbled, semi-industrial life of
fish-markets, lobsters, helicopters, and hovercraft, a crazy
logic of Alice-like grace.

'Catch' strikes me as a peculiarly contemporary poem, even
though at first glance it may look like one of the verbal games
played by sombre Victorian gentlemen like Lear and Dodgson.
Its self-containedness has a militant quality; for Finlay has
built into it the outlines of another kind of poem altogether.
Behind its facetiously ordered structure we can sense the
presence of a much more 'realistic', much more dour form—
an unrhymed, unmetrical exploration of the fate of the islander
about to be displaced by the coming of the machines. It
deliberately rejects that alternative, choosing instead the
quirky, fanciful world of rhymes and puns—a world in
which the poem is able to shake up and reconstruct its social
ingredients like so many bits of tinsel in a kaleidoscope.

In the last two or three years a surprising number of English
poets have been rediscovering doggerel as a form—a poetic
style in which rhymes are forced and metres crude, where the
cat's-cradle of structure is made to seem deliberately at odds

with the language that gets stuffed into it. George MacBeth's bawdy monologue 'The Painter's Model' is a very funny, and not uncomplicated, revamping of the techniques of graffiti, and of the kind of obscene verse that gets passed, in grubby typescript, from hand to hand in offices and factories:

> I was born in Rome from the yolk of eggs
> With a bit of mosaic between my legs.
>
> In Byzantium, I was plated and screwed
> Until they discovered *The Art of the Nude.*
>
> Van Eyck was an early performer in flesh,
> He laid me under a fine gold mesh.
>
> Hieronymus Bosch had a fertile mind,
> He blew me with a clarinet, from behind.
>
> Leonardo was a sadistic bleeder,
> I couldn't stand swans, so he made me Leda.
>
> Breughel was a vicious Flemish brute,
> I was varnished by him in my birthday suit.
>
> With Lucas Cranach, life was grim,
> There were gropes in water, and then a hymn . . .

And so on, through the history of art, to Picasso, Braque, Dali, and Jim Dine. Indeed, MacBeth's version of art history, though markedly extramural in tone, is savagely plausible— within earshot, at least, of Bernard Berenson and Herbert Read, and a good deal too close for comfort to those crib-book histories of Western painting in which artists are catalogued and described in terms which are, in their own way, no less vulgar than the painter's model's. The violently compressed order of doggerel, in which each couplet stands on its own, bound together by its blatant rhyme, becomes a mode of satiric commentary on other kinds of order—on the leisurely, indulgent connoisseurship of the art historian, on the machine-gun treatment of instant art history, and, ultimately, I suppose, on the way in which paintings themselves impose their

aesthetic ideologies on their human subjects. The reduction
in the scope of the language that doggerel enforces, along with
the jingling separatism of each couplet, gives the poem the
speed and the style of automatic caricature, of an accelerated
silent movie.

Elsewhere in his verse MacBeth has used riddles, number
codes, and borrowed European rhyme- and stanza-forms;
patterns which take on an autotelic power of their own—
means of reshaping and redistributing the kinds of public and
social experience which goes into his poetry. In his *Epistles*
(1970), from which I took the quotation that heads this
chapter, Donald Davie adopts a pseudo-Byronic doggerel in
order to conduct a fiercely witty quarrel with the conventions
of Black Mountain verse. Facetious rhymes and self-consciously pedantic syntax are made to provide an alternative
style of perception to the free-form, imitative, epic mode of
Olson and Dorn. And here, I think, the linguistic philosophy
of Wittgenstein's *Tractatus* and the Cambridge School has
been of immense importance in revivifying the possibilities of
imposed poetic structure. From Wittgenstein's famous dictum
that 'the limits of our language are the limits of our world' we
have learned that the essential nature of any statement is
fundamentally inseparable from the verbal form which it
takes. Or, putting in another way, the 'truth' of a poem cannot logically precede the way in which it is written.

> . . . is this a way
> To write, from now on quite uncouth
> Not qualified to tell the truth?

Davie's *Epistles*, which are really essays on the relationship of
history and poetic form, are obsessively concerned with
proving that 'truth' lies neither in the qualifications of the
versifier nor in the ultimacy of the space-time continuum, but
in the manner of saying. Taking the kind of historical figures
who in an Olson poem would turn out to be mythical space-
time heroes, like John Rae and Corporal John Ledyard, Davie

Byronizes them into so many Don Juans, having multifarious adventures in a doggerel string. It's a brilliant, professorial performance—a donnish tutorial on the arbitrary power of poetic form.

Not long ago Philip Larkin published what might look, to the unkind eye, like the Larkin poem to end all Larkin poems, 'Annus Mirabilis'; a doggerel invasion of his own wry, well-kept poetic apartment:

> Sexual intercourse began
> In nineteen sixty-three
> (Which was rather late for me)—
> Between the end of the *Chatterley* ban
> And the Beatles' first LP . . .

It functions as a kind of criticism-by-self-parody of Larkin's entire work, pushing the even rhymes, the confident metrics, the sharp darts of accurate social observation, and the lugubrious intrusions of a personal voice to the point of anarchic farce. Larkin, as a favourite target of the *New Statesman pasticheurs* on the Competition Page, has got his own back on his imitators; as a perfector of 'liberal' form he has given the form a chance to take over, and has proved it to be a more totalitarian style than even his denigrators might have expected. 'Annus Mirabilis' becomes a poem so promiscuous in its ironies that it turns into a maze, a stylistic labyrinth in which no directions are certain. In an odd way it satisfies all the impulses of rhyme and metre and syntax which are normally held in check: it allows them to exercise a radical oligarchy over the world of the poem. If we want to explain the over-bright tone, the sense of being bypassed, the underlying dejection, and the painful jokeyness of that first stanza of 'Annus Mirabilis' we shall have to refer, not to the caucus of liberal attitudes that we may imagine to cluster around Larkin's work, but to the stylistic form which enables them to exist. The manner has taken over the reins of the verse; the architectonics of the cat's-cradle dictate the size and sex of the baby.

4

The Politics of Poetic Structure

The time is gone, when *Pope* could ladle Wit
In couplet droplets, and decanter it.
Wordsworth's sweet broodings, *Milton's* pride,
And *Tennyson's* unease have all been tried;
Fin-de-siècle sickliness became
High-stepping Modernism, then went lame.
Art offers now, not cunning and exile,
But blank explosions and a hostile smile.

JOHN UPDIKE, 'Midpoint'

So far we have edged uneasily around the basic problems of the pluralism of contemporary verse. Imagine a large, rambling house, with every room decorated in a different style. In the basement a poetry rally is taking place; the audience are young, both English and American, and the noise is loud; a rock group plays during the intervals. In an upper room of the house an American lady talks to her analyst in a voice whose rhythms are broken by the strident irregularities of the nervous breakdown. Next door a group of Englishmen in tweed jackets chat politely to one another about the bric-à-brac of surburban life. A professor holds a seminar in the attic, and a Zen Master conducts devotional exercises around the kitchen table. In other rooms a variety of strangely dressed people wander disconsolately, addressing monologues to the furniture. Occasionally someone walking along the corridors taps on a door: 'Wouldn't you like to come and meet X?' he inquires. 'Thanks awfully, no,' or 'Beat it, man,' is the reply he gets. The house of poetry has been split up into flats; it has proliferated into a series of separate and mutually exclusive conceptual worlds.

Both poets and their critics have tried to get the occupants
of the house to come round a table and resolve their differences in a debate; they have constructed large dualisms to
explain the atmosphere of rancour and incomprehension that
clearly exists. The real split, we're told, is between the cosy
gentility of English verse as against the frontier audacity and
ambition of American writing (thus Al Alvarez). Or, according to Donald Davie, it is between poets who write within the
context of an established literary tradition and those who see
themselves as liberated innovators, free spirits who are able
to nod casually at history in the street without taking off their
hats. Donald M. Allen, in the preface to his influential
anthology *The New American Poetry*, ascribes it to the divide
between 'academic' verse and the poets who are in determined
revolt against the literary values of the university. We have
a situation in which the young are pitted against the old, the
English against the Americans, the provinces against the
urban centres, exponents of 'free form' against writers who
choose to work within an imposed structure, clerks against
bards, Aristotelian realists against Platonist inventors. If,
after the American fashion, one were to arrange a consortium
of poets, including, say, Philip Larkin, Charles Olson, Anne
Sexton, Adrian Henri, Ted Hughes, and Elizabeth Bishop, one
can imagine the awkward silences, the muttered disengage-
ments, the temporary embattled liaisons—the overall air of a
party which all the guests are anxious to leave early. For there
is no longer any gold standard to underpin the coinage of
contemporary poetics. Criticism has signally failed to relate
the disparate strands in recent verse, and poets themselves
have tended to pin their fortunes on the flags of partisan
ideologies. The language in which poetry is discussed has,
like the language of poetry itself, fragmented into a series—
or, more accurately, a jumble—of competing dialects.

We live in the aftermath of modernism—the last major
literary movement to achieve congruence between its political

and poetic styles. The profound conservatism of Eliot and Pound gave a wholeness and a coherence to their verse which has not been equalled since. Whether in seventeenth-century Europe or in mandarin China or in the France of the troubadours, these poets found a version of Eden from which their own century was seen to be the Fall. The villains of modernism —industrialism, secularism, Pound's Jewish usurers—were the serpents of this essentially neo-Christian mythology. There's a characteristic shift between Canto XIII and Canto XIV in *A Draft of XXX Cantos*, when Pound jumps from elegant *chinoiserie* to a hysterical denunciation of twentieth-century London and its government. In the XIIIth Canto he has Kung walking from the dynastic temple through a cedar grove, chatting in polite epigrams about the well-ordered state; in the XIVth Canto he is waxing crapulous, in a rhetorical stew of libellous obscenities:

> Above the hell-rot
> the great arse-hole,
>   broken with piles,
> hanging stalactites,
>   greasy as sky over Westminster,
> the invisible, many English,
>   the place lacking in interest,
> last squalor, utter decrepitude,
> the vice-crusaders, fahrting through silk,
>   waving the Christian symbols,
> . . . . . . frigging a tin penny whistle,
> Flies carrying news, harpies dripping shit through the air . . .

The poem itself is seen to be besmirched by the foulness of the world it catalogues; in the transition from canto to canto we exchange epigrams for curses, a balanced and formal syntax for an unruly string of expletives. But this is a style which needs a religion to support it; a vision of history which can locate the date of the Fall, which can give a meaning to blasphemy, and whose despair at man's present circumstances is constantly lit up by an accompanying belief in an ideal—

and essentially divine—order.

It is no accident that the literary voices of Eliot and Pound are prophetic, bardic, and priestlike. They are rooted in the Christian dualism of Eden versus the Fall, Man against God, the Past against the Present. Their version of the twentieth-century is the product of a theology of sin and pollution; and in their work the poem becomes an arena in which the two sides of the central dualism battle for supremacy. Indeed, the key terms of the New Criticism, the public-relations department of modernism, reflect just this obsession with the theological doubleness of experience: 'paradox', 'irony', 'ambiguity'—the figures of speech in which language itself can be seen to be riven by the Manichean struggle. In the ideology of modernism the poet's role was clearly defined as that of bard and soothsayer; the craggily isolated visionary standing in the detritus of a fallen world. It was a position of unprecedented elitism. It rejected the possibility of continuity, of a future, except in so far as it might yield a millennial holocaust, a Second Coming. The only kind of literary community it allowed was a licensed priesthood (for which, during the 1910s and 1920s, Ezra Pound acted as suffragan bishop, in the regrettable absence of the arch-prelate, Dante). The politics and economics of its poetic state were feudal in structure; all transactions were in gold, hierarchies established on the basis of blood-ties to selected ancestors (including Provençal balladeers, Villon, the Metaphysical poets, Shakespeare and Dante, the anonymous authors of certain Christian-Celtic legends, and the French Symbolists), and traditions reverenced with full ritual regalia and due dignity. For the fact that we have a body of twentieth-century verse of real stature, ambition, and complexity we have the modernist movement to thank; at the same time the ideology of modernism has subsequently proved a burden, like the ancient mariner's albatross, that more recent poets have found themselves forced to wear in unproductive penance.

For, since the 1930s, the overwhelming effort of contemporary verse has been concentrated on freeing the modern poem from the platform of Christian-conservatism to which the modernists had so firmly screwed it down. There has been a steady (if diverse and quarrelling) movement towards the democratization of the poem, towards finding a personal or local voice in which to phrase it, and towards allowing the poem to incorporate rather than resist the social and techno-logical change happening, with increasing pace, outside it. Correspondingly, assumptions about the nature of tradition and literary value, about the essential ontology of the poem, have been sometimes questioned, sometimes simply dumped, sometimes invented overnight to validate a new heterodoxy. As with politics at large, the most distinctive feature of con-temporary poetics has been the fight on very different fronts, to command the cultural centre; and even the revolu-tionary groups—the Beats, the Underground, and the militant regionalists—have both defined themselves against, and readily assented to, a mythical notion of 'centrality'.

This shift from elitism to centralism has been taking place almost continuously for forty years. William Carlos Williams opened the language and the structure of the poem to the democratic cross-currents of a provincial city and his doctor's practice, in an *œuvre* which works as a severe—and frequently enraged—critique of Eliot's verse and politics. But it is in the poetry of W. H. Auden that the implications of the shift have been most carefully and richly articulated. In a very early poem, written while he was still an undergraduate, the first published by John Fuller in his *Reader's Guide to W. H. Auden,* Auden fired a sharply comic warning shot over the bows of the kind of Christian dualism in which the verse of the 1920s was steeped:

> Tommy did as mother told him
>   Till his soul had split:
> One half thought of angels
>   And the other half of shit.

Auden himself, with considerable assistance from his enthu-

siasms for Icelandic sagas, revolutionary politics, and the
terminology of psycho-analysis, spent the 1930s firmly
resisting both mother and the millennial style of modernism.
Experimenting with verse-drama, ballads, blues, and traditional lyric forms, he worried at the language of the poem,
making it more demotic, more accessible to the small details
of domestic experience, more centred on the mortal, human
individual. There is, throughout his poetry, a constant
attempt to speak simultaneously of the large, public theme,
of 'ideas' as part of the natural discourse of the civilized man,
and of the tissue of minutiae which make up the hum and buzz
of ordinary life. The formal musicality of Auden's metrics
binds and guides a voice in which prophecy and chat sit side
by side. Favourite nursery words, like 'silly', 'clever', 'shoo',
dot his verse—pegs which pin down even the grandest and
newest notions that stalk in his poems. In a language so
brightly lit by common sense and common experience the
bardic posture becomes unavailable, or, at least, vulnerable
to the titter behind the hand, the banana-skin pratfall. In
'Musée des Beaux Arts' Auden points up the necessary
relationship between the contingent context of everyday
social life and the tragic or dramatic emotion which it frames:

> About suffering they were never wrong,
> The Old Masters: how well they understood
> Its human position; how it takes place
> While someone else is eating or opening a window or just
>   walking dully along;
> How, when the aged are reverently, passionately waiting
> For the miraculous birth, there always must be
> Children who did not specially want it to happen, skating
> On a pond at the edge of the wood:
> They never forgot
> That even the dreadful martyrdom must run its course
> Anyhow in a corner, some untidy spot
> Where the dogs go on with their doggy life and torturer's
>   horse
> Scratches its innocent behind on a tree.

Auden's poetry is deeply concerned with paying attention, with getting everything in; with the kind of unpresumptuous honesty of tone that comes from loosening and opening the poem to the populated middle-ground of society at large. It's an inherently anti-dualistic stance, and one that allows a basic democracy of perception within the diverse community of the poem's language. At the same time one needs to notice that the cumulative effect of all these inclusive gestures is to make a claim, not just for having, as it were, been fair to the facts of the case, but for having said everything there is to say —for nothing less than a comfortably omniscient wisdom. When Auden writes, in 1962, that

> The Holy Ghost
> does not abhor a golfer's·jargon,
> a Lower-Austrian accent, the cadences even
> of my own little Anglo-American
> musico-literary set . . .

it is hard to escape the corollary that the Holy Ghost actually prefers the cadences of Auden's own little musico-literary set. The geniality, the even casualness of phrase, itself becomes a bardic style. When Auden uses the first person he manages to make it stand for the entire body of reasonable men of sensibility. Anything outside the range of the particular inclusions of the poem becomes, by implication, silly or naughty. If Auden does sometimes sound like an old-fashioned nanny it is because the nursery—always a touchstone in his verse— has swelled to become the whole world.

Auden's verse powerfully enlists the reader as an enfranchised member of a democracy which turns out, on closer inspection, to be the nicest and kindest form of paternal dictatorship. We are able to use our votes only after the elections have taken place, yet we are persuaded that the decisions, the exclusions, the choices are all our own. This is the characteristic strategy of the poet claiming cultural centrality, for whom 'honesty' and 'directness' have become just as much fighting terms as the prophecy from the mountain was for the modernists.

Since the 1950s the movement towards centralism in English writing has involved a radical reinvention of literary tradition. Out have gone the French Symbolists ('*Foreign* poetry! No!', as Philip Larkin is on record as exclaiming); and in have come more avuncular ancestors, notably Thomas Hardy and Edward Thomas. What has been sought is a voice that has the authenticity and the authority of ordinariness; a language in which daily detail, low-key speech rhythms, and the experience and feeling of Rotherham rather than Byzantium add up to make a rhetoric with which the poem can deal face to face with the middling area of contemporary society. In the fifties Robert Conquest's anthology *New Lines* afforded a rostrum for the mild, centralist politics of the Movement poets. It is now rather too easy to dismiss the polite, self-deprecating tone of the *New Lines* contributors as an entirely becoming modesty; hard, perhaps, to see their struggle to restore the poem to an arena of social discourse in which the shared values of the post-war middle class could find a sensitive and flexible voice.

Indeed, the Movement and its successors (especially John Fuller, Ian Hamilton, David Harsent, Hugo Williams, and Douglas Dunn) have been most important for their creation of a mythology of realism; for giving a grammar and vocabulary, a series of locations and personae with which to construct a notional 'actuality'—an imaginary territory which the English reader can make tally with the privatization and provincialism of his sociological and political environment. Smallness, sparsity, fidelity to the sharp outlines of limited domestic experience compose an ideology of honesty in which the poem, as Peter Porter has remarked, is hardly allowed to begin to exist. Hugo Williams's 'The Couple Upstairs' might stand as a kind of fulcrum-point for British poetry in the late 1960s:

Shoes instead of slippers down the stairs,
She ran out with her clothes

And the front door banged and I saw her
Walking crookedly, like naked, to a car.

She was not always with him up there,
And yet they seemed inviolate, like us,
Our loves in sympathy. Her going

Thrills and frightens us. We come awake
And talk excitedly about ourselves, like guests.

This artfully tries to give the impression that it is not really
a poem at all. All the activity seems to be going on, not in the
language of the verse itself, but in the situation outside. The
flat narration of the first two stanzas, together with the
the deliberate grammatical *gaucherie* of that simile, 'like
naked', makes for a style in which the poet appears to be the
automatic recording-tool of his experience—a kind of typewriter on which the small disturbances of his world play
disjointedly across the keys. Williams habitually presents
himself as the unobserved observer—an immobile, invisible
figure who is only able to participate in the affairs he hears or
watches through minimal, sporadic bursts of imagination. In
the sparse context of 'The Couple Upstairs' a word like
'inviolate' comes to signify just as much imaginative labour
as half a dozen epic similes might for Milton.

This kind of modest acquiescence, where the poem becomes
an enactment of the writer's refusal to interfere with the world
outside, works as a kind of proof of the superior existence of
an external reality. The texture of the verse gets defined by
the degree to which it adheres or departs from a 'real' world
which, by implicit consensus, is known to be essentially
private, disjunctive, unplastic. By rejecting both the metaphysics and the rhetoric of the modernist movement a very
large number of recent, mainly English, writers have come to
depend heavily on a fictional version of reality which is

liberal, novelistic, and documentary in style. In an important
way they share the assumptions about society and language
that we have been more accustomed to in writers of prose
than in poets; a tradition of 'transparent' writing whose focal
figure is George Orwell and whose inheritors include Kingsley
Amis and Richard Hoggart. It is a style which springs from a
sense of the deeply felt necessity to speak straight, to cut
across the barriers of class and specialization and locality. It
is a style which has grown more insistent as society itself has
grown more diverse; it registers an ideal communicative
situation in which, even (or, rather, *especially*) in a divided
and pluralist culture, people can talk to one another in a
common, simple voice. Its source is autobiography: the form
in which the first person, and a sensitive fidelity to the facts
of an individual's experience, guarantees an authority of tone.
'Style', with its transforming tricks of metaphor and generalization, is kept subjugated to the irregular truths of 'experience';
the language of the poem is never allowed to stray far from
the narrow lines of language as it is used in the suburban
kitchen. Shared forms of experience—marriage, loneliness,
the fear of death, the routine of work, and all the slippery
trickles of insight and menace that intermit these—themselves
become the 'style' of the poem. Indeed, one sometimes senses
that there's an underlying conviction in the work of some of
our younger writers to the effect that the routinization of
modern urban and suburban life has created its own poetry.
The imprints of the same mass images, the same commuting
time-schemes, the same communal hopes and neuroses, have
given our lives so many shared versions of order and metaphor
that the poet's work is almost done for him; he becomes a
revealer, not a maker, teasing out the submerged logic of an
experience which we can recognize instantly as both our own
and everybody else's. Alan Brownjohn has written a fine
poem called 'A 202', which takes its whole style from the
meandering bric-à-brac of an arterial road in South London:

This coarse road, my road, struggles out
South-east across London, an exhausted
Grey zigzag of stubborn, unassimilable
    Macadam, passing hoardings pasted

With blow-ups of cricket journalists, blackened
And not-quite-Georgian terraces,
Shagged-out Greens of geraniums and
    Floral coats-of-arms, lost pieces

Of genteel facade behind and above
Lyons˙ shopfronts and 'Pullum Promotions',
—Journeying between wired-off bombed lots glossy
    With parked Consuls, making diversions

Round bus depots . . .

The poem itself becomes an exhausted catalogue of details and brand-names as it mimics the sludgy progress of the road; the metre is deliberately trailing and slack; the vocabulary is dully demotic. Unable to select, or discriminate between, its details, it moves like an indifferent mirror, suffocating in its own realism. Yet, undeniably, it talks in a common language in which the surface facts of contemporary social experience have a fixed place; its symbols are shared by every suburban driver of a clapped-out Ford. When Brownjohn ends the poem he pushes it towards a large aesthetic statement which seems to me to be crucial to the whole issue of centralism in recent verse:

. . . This road, generally, is one for
The long-defeated; and turns any ironic
Observer's tracer-isotope of ecology,
    Sociology, or hopeful manic

Verse into a kind of mere
Nosing virus itself. It leaves its despondent, foul
And intractable deposit on its own
Banks all the way like virtually all

Large rivers, particularly holy ones, which it
Is not. It sees little that deserves to be undespised.
It only means well in the worst of ways.
    How much of love is much less compromised?

'This road', the A 202, becomes as much a path of perception, a literary style, as it is a location on a street map. It stands, explicitly, for that mode of writing which deliberately compromises itself by submitting to the only common, available language that we have; a language that is 'realist' (in political as well as poetic terms), that belongs to the submerged and mortgaged middle class, that is promoted by property developers, television advertisements, feature-writers for popular newspapers, and politicians with the common touch. It is the language of Wilsonian pragmatism; a style in which facts and visible surfaces predominate; and in Brownjohn's poem it embodies a vital paradox. For on the one hand the existence of the poem—any poem—depends on the possibility of a common language in which experience can be shared, and, though heavy with irony, 'A 202' is a celebration of that possibility made fact for our own time. While on the other the peculiar quality of this common language turns the poem into a mere catalogue; straggling, broken-backed, cynically knowing. Is the compromise of love in the last line the product of the compromise of the language in which it takes place, or vice versa? Is, indeed, compromise—most desirable of liberal, 'realist' virtues—not something we should be thankful for?

The modest, regretful tone of the kind of 'British' English verse which American critics are so fond of attacking is rooted in the paradox explored by Brownjohn. If the function of the post-modernist poem is to return to the cultural centre, what can it find there—and can it still remain a poem? In social and political terms the notional centre of modern English and American life has become increasingly firmly defined; it is a threadbare cliché to observe that the rhetorics of both the Conservative and Labour parties and the Democrats and Republicans have moved much closer together—to cluster around the core of domestic, rather than foreign, or broad ideological, policy—in the period since World War II. This reflects a complex of facts, but, most importantly for my argument here, it mirrors the effect of a technology and a communications system which have been able to promote, with a success of quite alarming proportions, the values of a single style of middle-class life. Our language has distinctively changed as a result, and there is now, as poets have been— somewhat dejectedly—discovering, a 'midcult' (to borrow Dwight MacDonald's word) dialect in which the conventional suburban life, the conventional political opinion, the conventional cosmology, can be phrased.

American verse has a tradition of dissent which has made it noticeably less dependent than English writing on the powerful emergence of this common, central language. But one picks it up in the work of W. D. Snodgrass, who, like Philip Larkin, drives it towards Augustan parody and keeps his distance with self-mockery:

> The girls have grown so young by now
> I have to nudge myself to stare.
> This year they smile and mind me how
> My teeth are falling with my hair.
> In thirty years I may not get
> Younger, shrewder, or out of debt.
>
> The tenth time, just a year ago,
> I made myself a little list
> Of all the things I'd ought to know,
> Then told my parents, analyst,
> And everyone who's trusted me
> I'd be substantial, presently.

'April Inventory'

Snodgrass's domestic policy of making sharp, beautifully phrased, essentially *public* poems from his marriage and divorce and his work as a teacher is paralleled by the verse of Louis Simpson, W. S. Merwin, Elizabeth Bishop, even—

on occasions—Robert Lowell. There is a strong tendency to cultural centralism in American poetry (indeed, Robert Frost, long before the advent of the Nixon-Agnew administration, was habitually, though mistakenly, taken for a genial, homy spokesman for the silent majority), even though the literary radicals, in their revolt from it, have found it hard to pin down and have taken frequent refuge in vague apostrophes to 'academic' verse.

For just as the centre has congealed in Anglo-American culture, so the right and the left have moved farther apart, defining themselves not against each other but against the consensus in the middle. And certainly the most spectacular energies in recent verse have been devoted to kicking against the common, middle-class language of the cultural centre. The pluralism of modern poetics that I sketched at the beginning of this chapter is not explicable in terms of either dialogues or dualisms; for it is the expression of radical extremes and alternatives, posed against a centre which, by definition, is shifting, amorphous, vague, able to assimilate all but the most tendentious arguments and attitudes. The soggy grip of centralism has forced the poet who is not prepared to work within it (or at least attack it from within, by parody, or extension to absurdity) to adopt a revolutionary, or arch-conservative, or totalitarian style.

Consider, in this context, three examples taken from poems which, however different in their styles, share a violent resistance to the politics and poetics of centralism—a violence that shows itself primarily in the extremity of the rhetorical and syntactical gestures to which they have access.

> Walter Llywarch! The words were the name
> On a lost letter that never came
> For one who waited in the long queue
> Of life that wound through a Welsh valley.
> I took instead, as others had done
> Before, a wife from the back pew
> In chapel, rather to share the rain

Of winter evenings than to intrude
On her pale body. And yet we lay
For warmth together and laughed to hear
Each new child's cry of despair.

'Walter Llywarch', R. S. THOMAS

Lifesize jellybabies shaped like Hayley Mills
A black-and-red flag flying over Parliament
I want to paint
Every car crash on all the motorways of England
Père Ubu drunk at 11 o'clock at night on Lime Street
A SYSTEMATIC DERANGEMENT OF ALL THE SENSES
In black running letters 50 miles high over Liverpool

I want to paint
Pictures that children can play hopscotch on
Pictures that can be used as evidence at Murder trials
Pictures that can be used to advertise cornflakes
Pictures that can be used to frighten naughty children
Pictures worth their weight in money
Pictures that tramps can live in
Pictures that children would find in their stockings on
        Christmas morning
Pictures that teenage lovers can send each other
I want to paint
              pictures.

'I Want to Paint', ADRIAN HENRI

Here we have it—the goods—from this Harbour,
1626, to Weymouth (England) consigned to

     Richard Bushrod and Company
     & Wm Derby and Company

fr Cape An   dry fish

corfish

train oil

quarters of oak

```
skins:      fox
          racons
          martyns
           otter
       muskautche
          beaver
```

          The *Amytie* arriving Weymouth 1st Aug
          and the *Fellowship* following 11th September
          Capts Evans, & Edward Cribbe

                              Maximus, CHARLES OLSON

Thomas's Wales, Henri's Liverpool, and Olson's Gloucester, Massachusetts, all provide eccentric vantage-points—places where all sorts of things are possible that are undreamed of in the suburban kitchen or on the A 202. The bleak, unqualified baldness of Thomas's metaphors, and the radical paradox of the final line of the poem, with its echo of Blake's 'London', grow naturally out of a landscape and language in which human life has been simplified and foreshortened to the cold, scratched existence of the rural peasant. Death, hunger, isolation, the primordial repetitions of a life that swings on a mean axis between chapel and hill-farm, are allowed to confront one another within the poem, in a syntax that has been stripped nearly naked. The dramatic invocation, the reduction of a whole lifetime to a single metaphor, and of all the complications of marriage and childbirth to a blunt and negative reason, are made possible by the poem's immersion in a culture which can act, at best, only as an analogy for most people's experience of living in the twentieth century. 'Wales' becomes a special, spare grammar and vocabulary in which certain statements can be made as in no other language.

Equally, Olson's Weymouth port book and Henri's child-like, Liverpudlian voice (the voice, in fact, of a child who skips in his reading from *Batman* comics to the manifestos of European surrealism and post-expressionism) offer arrangements of words, jumps in time and space, and wild rhetorical possibilities that are denied in the central language of the culture. These poems work through their oddity; they assault the conventional hierarchies and categories of everyday language by a process of inversion, obliquity, and humour. The asyntactical catalogue (in both Henri and Olson) is set up as an alternative to the qualified logic of suburbia's careful grammar. Antiquarianism and the pop collage are used to subvert the realist world of here-and-now, of *but* and *because*. A style of incantation (in Adrian Henri, who is endlessly fond of constructing primary-coloured litanies) and the arrangement of the poem on the page (in Olson, whose typographical imagination, as here, is always visually subtle and satisfying) transport the verse to a position of radical extremity from the middle ground of the cultural centre.

Yet I think it's fair to say that it is the centre that enables poems like these to adopt such strategies of dissent and alienation. The myth of Bohemia has been revived, to provide an even firmer footing for the poet than if offered in the nineteenth century. The centre is now strong enough (due to circumstances quite outside poetry) to support a whole army of gipsy irregulars at its perimeters. As individuals all they have in common is protest and resistance; and it's no coincidence that one of the most—well, almost—respectable poetry magazines in the United States should be called *Fuck You*. Whether their particular slice of the perimeter is located in Black Mountain, or Wales, on Haight-Ashbury, or even on the campus, it affords a view that is bound, on the one side, by the centre itself and, on the other, by the radical alternative offered by its own special position. We are confronted by militant provincialism, militant historicism, militant experimentalism. Even the centre itself shows signs, in the current jargon, of being radicalized by obsessive self-parody. The politics of poetry have shifted, from the liberal consensus of the nineteenth century and the embattled conservatism of the modernists, to a confused and frequently vituperative pamphlet war between the centre and its extremes.

5

Tradition and Value: The Poem in a Mixed Culture

'HAIL TO ALL EDGES'
Placard put up by Ken Kesey's Pranksters

As the new bohemians have lit out from the cultural centre they have engineered a scatter phenomenon in contemporary poetics. This has brought in its wake an all-out attack on literary tradition, on the territorial boundaries between 'life' and 'art' on which most of our conventional aesthetic maps have been based, on elitist assumptions of poetic value, and even on history itself, as the medium through which canons of social and literary style are communicated. In the attempt to uproot the poem from the topsoil of its middle-class, continuous, historical context society has been ransacked for forms and styles which are free of the burden of a centralist tradition. Jazz, pop music, drugs, political protest, the image of the poet as troubadour rather than as craftsman-intellectual, have provided a series of analogies for the poetry of dissent. All of them offer styles—of language, social behaviour, and cosmology—in which the poem can walk in new, if borrowed, clothes. When Allen Ginsberg syncopates, in 'Seabattle of Salamis Took Place off Perama',

> Hail to the noise wherever the jukebox is on TOO LOUD
> that the Muses are loose in the world again with
>   their big black voices and bazookey blues . . .
> Apocalypse Rock, Open the Door Richard, I'm casting
>   A Spell On You, End of History Rag!

the style of the funky jazzman provides a whole vocabulary of subversion and protest. It gives Ginsberg a vicarious tradition of black rather than white culture, with antecedents in African not European forms; a putative 'cat' in the counter-world of gigs and fixes, where the poetry of T. S. Eliot is not so much rejected as non-existent. One needs to ask, I think, just why people like Ginsberg have needed to borrow such extreme, and often ill-fitting, masks; why the voice of litera-ture itself and its tradition in Western culture has been so blandly indentified with the despised class of parents and policemen.

It is a question that can only be answered by looking for a while at the basic nature of those highly selective institutions to which we conventionally attach the label of 'tradition'. When Eliot and Leavis (in, say, 'Tradition and Individual Talent' and *The Great Tradition*) use the word, it denotes a closed value-system; a poetic economy in which the currency is fixed by a particular theory of literary worth and in which the status of individual members is determined by the amount of capital each possesses. In any one tradition the majority of poets living and dead will be relegated to the proletarian mass since they will be seen to possess only a pocketful of petty cash in the right currency. In Leavis's system the pound sterling roughly corresponds to 'a whole response to Life' and 'a sanitive influence on the culture'. In Eliot's system the coinage is more sophisticated and finely minted; its numerous denominations include 'a historical imagination', 'a capacity for impersonality', and the ability to weld together a variety of diverse thoughts and feelings into a single 'complex'.

If we look at the actual make-up of the elites in both Eliot's and Leavis's traditions we find that they have a curious, essentially social, congruence. Leavis's has the air of a deter-minedly free-thinking, anti-aristocratic Cambridge party. George Eliot is there, despite rumours about her private life and her aggressively blue-stocking manner. So is Conrad, another rather over-serious person who talks in a faintly European accent. Indeed, the most celebrated guest, around whom nearly all the conversation revolves, is D. H. Lawrence, with his flat vowels, earnestly preaching his theology of sex and the truth of the blood, in the bluntest of terms. Leavis's tradition is a meritocratic elite; middle class, self-made, a little humourless. By contrast, Eliot's looks like the kind of cultivated soirée that might be assembled in a London or Paris drawing-room. Dante chats to Shakespeare; Laforgue and John Donne converse in French; Aristotle and Dryden engage in animated discussion about the function of criticism. The overall tone is one of ironical wit, of assured greatness without strain or condescension. It is a gathering of the natural aristocrats of letters.

But one of the essential functions of a tradition is that it is not an entirely static system; within the limits imposed by the nature of its particular currency, it can be manipulated, opened to new members, closed to others. A good, workable tradition on the Eliot/Leavis model provides a continuously fluid guest-list, on which additions and deletions can be worked by an arrangement of tariffs and quotas. Eliot expelled Milton in the 1920s, only to reintroduce him as guest of honour in the 1940s; in *The Great Tradition* Leavis announced that Dickens did not quite qualify for admission to his top-drawer party ('The adult mind doesn't as a rule find in Dickens a challenge to an unusual and sustained seriousness'), but in 1970 he and Mrs Leavis were graciously pleased to install Dickens before their own fireplace. ('Charles Dickens . . . David Lawrence. We're sure you'll both find a great deal in common.') Such changes of mind (Leslie Fiedler, unkindly, has called them 'deathbed repentances') work as valuable public proofs of the elasticity, the essential reality, of the system itself.

This image of a tradition as a social and economic system is more than just a flippant cartoon, although, of course, I have hardened its edges to make the point; it does correspond at a very deep level indeed to a basic habit of mind which we tend to adopt when we think about literature. Our terms for organizing the profusion of particular works of art into manageable patterns and hierarchies are drawn directly from our experience as members of an economically stratified society. 'Value', 'greatness', 'worth', 'richness', 'substance' (all words drawn from the first chapter of *The Great Tradition*), are metaphors of a very explicit kind, and we should not forget it. So, indeed, are 'vulgar' and 'cultivated', two more of Dr Leavis's favourite words. When we talk about aesthetics we are likely to find it impossible to do more than merely reflect our assumptions about society; and the particular tradition, or theory of poetic value, tends to enshrine the whole caucus of prevalent attitudes in the society—and the subculture—in which it is formulated. If the two traditions of Leavis and Eliot bear a striking resemblance to two conflicting social groups of a very recognizable kind—the meritocratic versus the aristocratic—that, of course, in no way discredits them; but it does help to explain why recent attacks on them have been phrased in a rhetoric that is more social than purely literary.

For a closed aesthetic system of the kind represented by these 'traditions' corresponds to a certain kind of closed social structure. The categoric distinctions which they impose between 'literature' and 'non-literature', and between 'excellence' and 'mediocrity', function best if we are able to imagine the individual work as a commodity in search of a fixed value in the literary economy. Prices get established on the basis of demand ('relevance', or the complex of supposed social necessities that Leavis indicates when he calls a work 'significant') and scarcity (and here one notices the radical difference between the value attached to 'originality' in Western culture as against its relative unimportance in most folk art or the culture of contemporary China). At the same time we believe that value somehow resides in the intrinsic nature of the work itself; as we say, it 'transcends' the shifting currents of its audience's whims, needs, and spending power. It is around this paradox, in which the poem is seen as both *of the world* and *beyond the world*, that nearly every major theoretical argument in criticism and aesthetics has revolved. And one of the essential functions of a 'tradition' and the 'critical standards' it entails is to mediate between the two sides of the paradox; to provide a frame of social references and values in which to locate the elusive, quasi-mystical nature of the work itself.

But the particular traditions and standards which we have inherited are instinct with the assumptions and values of a society which has itself recently come in for tough questioning and assault; and there has been a widespread feeling that society can no longer be quarrelled with in its own terms—the New Left, at any rate, have insisted that the only way to attack a society you hate is to adopt rhetorics and forms from outside it. In politics this has meant a style of slogans rather than arguments, of demonstrations rather than debates; it has meant the use of tactical obscenity and a kind of deliberate childishness in which the comic strip takes over from *Hansard* as a medium of political communication. The established channels and institutions are held to be so polluted by the messages that have already passed through them that they have become the automatic printing-presses of a corrupt society. The Chicago 'conspiracy' trial, in which Abbie Hoffman, Bobby Seale, and others attempted to sabotage court procedures by a mixture of burlesque, protesting declamation, and nursery pranks, provides an exact model for a certain kind of contemporary style in both literature and the community at large. For literature (in the sense of a continuing tradition in English and American writing), like the courtroom, can be seen as an institution whose forms can only endlessly mirror and repeat the old, bad structures of the society to which it belongs.

By the 1950s British poetry had come to seem inextricably rooted in a social establishment and centre that was rapidly turning into an uninhabitable house. Even though its means of transmission had already been decentralized, thanks to such enterprising ventures as the Hand and Flower Press and the Marvell Press, its audience was largely composed of a sector of the conventionally educated elite; its language was timidly and self-consciously 'traditional', tempered by the constraints and suggestions of academic criticism. Looking now at most of the poems in *New Lines* or in Al Alvarez's anthology, *The New Poetry*, it is easy to agree that poetry, at least once in the recent past, did become as much a stable social 'institution' as the High Street family business.

No wonder, then, that pop music afforded such an enticing counter-analogue to the institutionalization of poetry and its language; for here was a form whose audience cut straight across the social hierarchy, whose values were fluid and independent of any socially or historically based tradition, whose styles were vividly anti-centralist, with their insistent rhetoric of hallucinogenic experience, sexual liberty, and the ideology of being young—a language in which to be, with the Beatles, aged sixty-four was an unlikely joke. The pop concert, with its emphasis on the moment of performance (the music was not an impersonal product to be conveyed from the artist to the audience; it happened, as when the Who smashed up their electronic equipment, as part of the total dynamics of the situation itself), was a model of what poetry had ceased to be; a democratic event involving a great deal of collaboration between audience and performers, a social experience in its own right, relatively free from the conventions and structures of society outside. What is more, pop music was appropriating many of the traditional functions of poetry. During the 1960s it became standard practice to print the words of the lyrics on record sleeves; and certainly when the Beatles' *Sergeant Pepper's Lonely Hearts Club Band* appeared, songs like 'A Day in the Life' were heard and read as poems. Bob Dylan, and his expurgated English edition, Donovan, along with Leonard Cohen, Simon and Garfunkel, the Doors, the Who, and the Procul Harum, all poeticized their lyrics with weird and wonderful devices: violent antitheses (like Cohen's hideously coy 'I will kill you if I can . . . I will help you if I must'), home-

made romantic 'imagery', elaborately fey and violent metaphors, and pieces of extraordinary pastiche, like the Doors'
version of classical verse (Homer? Shakespeare? Milton?) in
'Horse Latitudes':

> When the still sea conspires an armour
> And her sullen and aborted
> Currents breed tiny monsters,
> True sailing is dead.

In fact, if one leafs through Richard Goldstein's anthology,
The Poetry of Rock, what is most striking is the poetic con-
ventionality of most of the lyrics; a good many of the lines
from Dylan, Cohen, and Simon and Garfunkel, for instance,
could just as easily be attributed to Ella Wheeler Wilcox.
What distinguishes them is their means of transmission; and,
ironically enough, pop audiences are responding extrava-
gantly to words and sentiments which, in the context of an
established publisher's list or the verse fill-in space in *The
Listener* or *New Statesman*, they would—not unjustly—pour
scorn on.

From experiments in the late fifties and early sixties with
concerts of poetry and jazz (where the voice, as it followed
the rhythm and melodic line of the music, appropriated the
'words on the page' instead of merely rendering them, as
straight readings tended to do), and from the sudden upsurge
of political balladry, sparked off by the Aldermaston marches
and fostered by new poets like Christopher Logue and Adrian
Mitchell, at least one branch of English verse moved further
and further into the dimension of performance. The Albert
Hall 'Poetry International' festival of 1965 (see Edwin
Morgan's astronautical celebration of the event, quoted in
Chapter 2) was poetry's first pop concert; its troubadour
performers set a style which was to be echoed in a growing
rash of public readings around the country. By 1970 a large
number of poets had grown accustomed to trekking, like beat
groups, to one-night stands in provincial towns (sometimes,

even, taking with them, like Bob Cobbing, an array of electronic equipment that a pop group might envy); and, once
there, they read, or declaimed, or, like Bob Cobbing, gurgled,
to an audience whose parish magazine was the *International
Times*, who found no inconsistency in flipping from the music
of, say, the Beatles or the Cream to the poetry of Adrian
Mitchell, Roger McGough, Adrian Henri, or Tom Pickard.
Indeed, the distinction between poetry and pop has in some
quarters been so blurred by cross-movements between the
two that it has effectively ceased to exist. The Scaffold started
off in late night revue (with a show on Granada TV), performed
poems in pubs and students' unions, took their record 'Lily
The Pink' into the Top Ten, and established a style in which
satire, verse, and popsong could be simultaneously maintained within the same group identity. Adrian Henri, Pete
Brown, Tom Pickard, Henry Graham, amongst others, have all
doubled as musician-poets; they have converged to make a
very substantial attack upon the opposition between 'high
art' and pop, in a movement that has been self-consciously
anti-elitist.

But what is most interesting about the rapid growth of
poetry-as-performance is the new aesthetic which it has in
part created, in part affiliated itself to. Much earlier in the
century Tristan Tzara, André Breton, and Anton von Webern
(the mentor of Stockhausen, the only 'serious' composer who
figures on the cover of *Sergeant Pepper*) tried, in Dada,
surrealism, and serial music, to savage the categoric rigidity
of the line between art and non-art; to bring the poem,
painting, or composition into the temporal realm of events
rather than the spatial world of objects. An event is not
reproducible (it may, at best, only be imitated); and if the
economy of the conventional artistic 'tradition' assumes that
works of art are consumer durables whose value is located
not in passing time but in the static order of history, art
as an event subverts the most basic of all our socio-critical
categories. Furthermore, since an event implicates all its

participants (the bystander as much as the corpse and the policeman), one cannot separate out the 'work itself' from either the 'author' who performs it or from the 'audience' whose participatory response has become an essential ingredient of the total experience. If we are going to be able to talk adequately in its own terms of the poetry event we shall have to find a critical vocabulary which will stretch to describing, not 'the poem' as a fixed, transcendent entity, but 'what happened at the Round House between the hours of . . . on x date'.

George MacBeth, who has himself moved fluidly from a centralist stance in the 1950s to his current position as exponent, critic, and publicist of the new radical verse, calls the poetry event, 'a new work created out of pre-existent materials'. These materials include not only the written or printed texts of poems, but also the physical presence of the audience and the web of expectations and values they bring with them, the particular characteristics of the environment in which the event takes place (the size, lighting, seating arrangements, and acoustic properties of the hall), and the styles of performance which the other poets bring to the event. In this complicated chemistry everything that takes place, from the rain on the roof to the poet's tobacco cough to the lady who faints in the aisle, becomes absorbed into the total structure. As MacBeth interestingly observes, when the poet's introductory patter is relatively formal, and his poem is phrased in a conversational doggerel, the patter itself is likely to take on the air of poetry. Meanwhile the audience's silence, laughter, and degree of attention shape the poem; the speed and emphasis of its delivery alters, stanzas can be cut or rearranged to suit the changing mood of the event. With poems written for occasions like this, the audience can be brought in, pantomime-fashion, to speak choric lines; in one poem in his *Orlando* sequence MacBeth has his listeners all shouting out, 'Help!' Would that more poets allowed us the same liberty.

An event, because it happens in time rather than history,

has chance as its prime determinant. It represents a collision of circumstances without the inhering order imposed by an authoritative point of view, by the detached surveillance of memory, or by the otherness of print whereby the poem ceases to be a process of composition and turns into an object. In all these ways the notion of poetry-as-an-event conflicts violently with our customary assumptions about tradition and value. It cannot be satisfactorily viewed as an object, since each performer and individual member of the audience is likely to find it a different object; it cannot be transmitted intact from one time-sequence to another; the currency in which its value is expressed is like Monopoly money—it lasts strictly for the duration of the game. Attempts at direct re-production—by tape-recorders, films, or TV cameras—can record, at most, only a very limited number of audial- and view-points when the event, by definition is composed of the constantly changing responses of every one of its participants.

Let me illustrate, since really it's the only fair way to do it, from personal experience. In the summer of 1968 Bob Cobbing, complete with portable technology, went to Norwich to deliver a selection of his sound-poems, and to join a local group, the Australian Dancers, in some ritual incantation. The event took place on the upper floor of a once beautiful, but now semi-derelict, Elizabethan house in the centre of the city. The acoustics had the odd emptiness of a deserted wooden building; and the audience—a mixture of the local hip fringe and well-barbered and tweeded poetry-lovers who hadn't realized what they were letting themselves in for—were a good deal cowed, both by each other and by the dusty stately-home atmosphere in which they found themselves. People sat around on the floor, some of them clutching beer-bottles a little embarrassedly. Cobbing's net-work of amplifiers and trailing leads looked—and sounded—quite extraordinary in their decrepit, old-world context. When the poems started one felt the thin wooden boarding of the floor buzz under one; electronic whines and howls were interspersed with the products of Cobbing's incredible vocal reservoir. At the end of each performance there was a long, expectant silence, then the shorn members of the audience began to clap, politely; followed, seconds later, by clapping in more satirical vein, from the jeaned and belled section, who obviously found the behaviour of the clerks and grammar-school teachers just as entertaining as Cobbing's poems. Sensitized to noise generally, by the oddity of those noises officially designated as 'poetry', one began to respond to the pattern of clapping, coughs, whispers, and the steady tramps of shoes on wood as the lady form-mistresses took themselves elsewhere, on the same level. Lighting cigarettes, I found myself striking matches at points of rhythmical emphasis; and the complex of contingent sounds began to resolve themselves around the basic shapes of Cobbing's poems. In the intervals between 'poems', talking to a girl friend, we both became suddenly self-conscious at the sounds of our own voices and the conversation stopped. I don't know Bob Cobbing, but I'm sure he would have been delighted; the evening, in its own terms, was a spectacular success, compounded of incongruity, embarrassment—a fragmented sound pattern which worked as a trenchant image of something very much larger than the contained two-hour stretch of that particular night.

In this sense I find it hard to agree with John Cage, who, speaking on behalf of the new avant-garde in the regal 'we', told Frank Kermode in a B.B.C. interview for the series 'Is an Elite Necessary' (October–November 1970):

> I wouldn't say that we are interested in destroying the barrier between art and life or even blurring it. I would say we are interested in observing there is no barrier between the two.

No *formal* barrier between the two, admittedly; but there is a real and important temporal one. The poem or the piece of music viewed as an event is marked by the two points of its commencement and its ending; a slice of time which has a very special authority of focus. Hours and minutes provide just as rigid a frame for the work as the gold-leaf and papier-mâché (or the margins of the printed page) do for the more traditional version of the object in space. The poem-as-event performs an implicit commentary upon all the other events which compose our lives; we are allowed, for a finite period of time, to respond fully to all the contingencies which, under normal circumstances, we need to censor. The flickering patterns of chance become dramatically exposed, lifted free from their usual encasement in a web of ordering categories and hierarchies.

At this point people who have attended a few large-scale poetry events will no doubt be losing their patience. For on very few occasions (and then only sporadically) have these affairs come anywhere near to realizing the large formal claims that I have been making for them. Alvarez's testy dismissal of the poetry concert as an exercise in populariza-tion and seduction by flinging 'diluted near-verse' at a mass audience (in *Beyond All This Fiddle*) is not an unjust descrip-tion of what has actually tended to occur; and the prospect of poets traipsing humbly and hopefully in the wake of Dylan and the Rolling Stones has made a picture whose watery colours have run with more dumb pathos than innovatory energy. What is important is that a handful of writer-per-formers—Olson, Creeley, Dorn, Tom Raworth, MacBeth, Henri—have begun on a sophisticated exploration of audial and temporal space. Can one break down the traditional bar-riers between the poem, its author, and its audience? Can a poem, like a car crash, 'happen'? How well, or how badly, do traditional notions of poetic value work when the poem be-comes an event rather than an object? Is 'the event' a success-ful metaphor for the kind of continuous, open field of ex-perience which many have proposed as an alternative to the categoric, dualistic frame which Christianized, Western culture inherited from its past? By rejecting the notion of poem-as-object is it possible to set it free from our commodity-centred artistic economy, which is itself a product of a certain style of capitalist, middle-class life?

It's essential to raise those questions in that kind of machine-gun barrage; they are the haunting, unanswered, partially explored ultimates of contemporary verse, and their bold seriousness is not easily pegged down to neat clauses and subdivisions. They are, I believe, deeply embedded in the current outbreak of poetry readings and concerts, even if so many of these occasions have fallen shy of the questions they have raised. Behind the alarmingly casual chat (one can overhear it any day on the steps of the Round House) about the democratization of art, and, like, we're done with categories, man, and god I get so bugged with critical *values*, there is a hard core of extremely important specifics. And academic commentators have been ignoring them for far too long, on the sympathetic, but untenable, grounds that if the manner in which they are presented is so slickly disagreeable the matter can hardly be worth bothering about either.

But if the public poetry event has been the most florid outgrowth of this sequence of questions and possibilities, the poem on the page has also been pushing hard against the spatial objectification imposed by print. The notion of the poem as a process, a happening, with all the social and aesthetic implications which that implies, has been centred, not on the act of transmission, but on the activity of composition. Putting words down on paper—arranging language as it occurs during the time in which the poem is *made*—has become the primary topic of a great deal of recent verse. What, for instance, does one do with a concrete poem like this one, by Stuart Mills?

The sea is

There are three words missing from the above sentence. Choose three from the following list and complete it.

very long extremely tall quite deep often today

The 'reader' of this poem becomes its 'author' if he follows the rules of the game; the poem is made to happen afresh every time someone picks a new combination to finish the sentence. And the instant possibilities available range from the dully literal ('The sea is often extremely deep') to the surrealistically bizarre ('The sea is quite extremely tall') or the ungrammatically obscure ('The sea is very quite today'). Although the writer structures the event of the poem within certain finite limits, the poem occurs while the reader programmes his choice or choices through its computer-like mechanism. Is it a 'good poem'? Or is, say, 'The sea is quite extremely tall' a 'better poem' than, say, 'The sea is often extremely deep'? And since they are both the same poem, we are left in a position in which the poet has, like Stephen Dedalus's figure of the artist, gone off to pare his fingernails behind the scenes of the artifice for which he was originally responsible; we look in vain for the authority of the author.

This retreat from authority—whether it is the authority of the artist or the authority of a tradition—has found a crucial image in the impersonal randomization of the computer. An electronic system embodies in itself no values, and its past can be instantly obliterated by feeding it a new programme. John Cage, who has spent the last two decades in a tireless and obsessive campaign to set his works free from his own artistic dictatorship, has fed the random-selection process of the *I Ching* into a computer, and used the resulting print-out to determine the placing of words and musical sounds in his compositions. Edwin Morgan has carried the process one stage further and wittily 'computerized' John Cage; in his poem 'Opening The Cage' he takes a Cage quotation, 'I have nothing to say and I am saying it and that is poetry', and arranges it into fourteen variations on the fourteen words:

> I have to say poetry and is that nothing and am I saying it
> I am and I have poetry to say and is that nothing saying it
> I am nothing and I have poetry to say and that is saying it
> I that am saying poetry have nothing and it is I and to say
> . . .

—and so on. The point is that language happens here not as the result of the imposition of the hierarchy of imagination, but as a series of possibilities made available by the application of a set of impersonal rules. The chance statements, images, and collisions all occur as 'events'—the results of a dice game played with the movable properties of language. In this context all the resources of verse—puns, rhymes, metrics, assonances—can be assembled as materials for a game in which everything that happens (and we are significantly close here to Wittgenstein's phrase, *everything that is the case*), like the contingent noise at a poetry reading, becomes assimilated into the poem. Christopher Middleton passes a newspaper headline in 'The Joke':

> nun found nude on dunes
> nun found stunned on dunes at noon
> nude nun found stunned at noon
> nude nun on dunes had been stunned & screwed
>
> who saw nun stand scanning dunes?
> who stunned nun?
> who denuded stunned nun?
> who screwed nude stunned nun on dunes? . . .

All these attempts to turn the poem into an event or a process hinge around a central proposition: that the rules of language, like the rules of reality, are essentially impersonal; that any combination they may produce will be just as 'valid' as any other combination; that we live in a world composed of infinite possibilities rather than a closed, Manichean universe of good and evil, correct and incorrect. Only time dictates the scope and limits of our activity; and, to quote the supremely indifferent hero of John Barth's novel *The End of the Road*, echoing Wittgenstein, 'everything is that is the case'.

Nor should we miss the chilling implications of experiments like these, for they point towards a condition where literature and art become ultimately superfluous, or perhaps where life itself achieves the freedom—and the impersonality—of the work of art. They constitute a kind of prophetic science fiction; depending on how you look at it, a nightmarish, or utopian, version of a total universe. The world they predicate, whatever may be said in the studios of Hampstead or Berkeley, hasn't yet come into being; they are essays on a future freedom which all our cultural and social inheritance conspires to prevent us from exercising. In the smoke and dimmed lights of a poetry reading we may believe for a moment that we've arrived, but the networks of order and authority, of value and tradition, reimpose themselves as soon as we get out again into the street. But this shadowed future has made the practice of conventional social and literary styles more cautious and more anguished; even in the work of writers who evidently shrink from the abandoned universe of Cage and his fellows, like Philip Larkin and Robert Lowell, one can hear the accelerated pulse-rate of a body tensing itself before the threat of a future which is as yet only a series of apprehensions.

6

Words Alone

Cut right through the pages of any book or newsprint—
lengthwise, for example—and shuffle the text. Put them
together at random and read the newly constituted
message. Do it for yourself. Use any system which suggests
itself to you. Take your own words or the words said
to be 'the very own words' of anyone else living or dead.
You'll soon see that words don't belong to anyone. Words
have a vitality of their own and you or anybody can make
them gush into action . . . The poets are supposed to liberate
the words—not to chain them into phrases. Who told poets
they were supposed to think? . . . Writers don't own their
words. Since when do words belong to anybody? 'Your very
own words' indeed! And who are 'you'?

BRION GYSIN, 'Statement on the cutup
method and permutated poems'

His policy of defoliation
Gave Concrete Poetry to the nation.

PETER PORTER, 'Applause for Death'

Despite the ingenuous reasoning of Marshall McLuhan, we
live in a world whose new media have promoted more
language than any previous culture has had to live with. Its
sheer bulk surrounds, and assaults, and whispers to us daily;
in advertisements, newspaper headlines, packaging, slogans
commercial and political, billboards, film and TV titles; the
graphics industry enjoys a continuous boom. Significantly,
one of the latest fads in the automobile-accessory craze is the
sale of transfers with which you can print the brand name of
your car in enormous letters along its wing. We inhabit a kind
of total environmental collage of words, written and spoken

in a confusing plethora of dialects. In an important sense we have, during this century, witnessed the passing of language from the hands of the community into the transmission devices of the communicators. Indeed, 'communications' have become, quite literally, an 'industry'. It is now possible, as never before, for the individual to be alienated from the forms of his own language; a hostile stranger to the very means which afford him his existence as a social being.

The roots of this situation lie deep in the field of socio-linguistics. Sufficient here to remark that, until a quite recent phase of history, language was transmitted on an oral, class basis; both the yeoman and the squire acquired a range of vocabulary and a series of syntactical possibilities that were consonant with their particular social experience. The French structural linguist Ferdinand De Saussure made a central distinction here when he divided functions of language into *langue* and *parole*. *Langue* comprises the entire repertoire of rules and components in a single language; it represents both the source and the theoretically infinite total of uses to which the language can be put. *Parole* is the specific utterance, the example of the rules at work in a particular situation, the item in the repertoire. In a pre-industrial society, had one been able to record every linguistic usage that an individual spoke or heard, wrote or read (his personal *parole*), during his lifetime, they would have an essentially social coherence. Examples of incomprehension (a piece of whimsical, aristocratic circumlocution overheard by a tradesman, perhaps) would be explicable—provided they operated within the rules afforded by the *langue* and weren't the ungrammatical utterances of the psychotic—in terms of social distance.

But in the sort of industrial society we inhabit language can be treated like any other natural resource; commodities can be manufactured from it which bear no relationship to social need. The potentials of the *langue* are ransacked to provide instances of *parole* which are the plaster ducks and aluminium models of the Eiffel Tower of the communications world;

gratuitous, mass-produced objects that have no function except to titillate the consumer into keeping the commercial wheels turning. The syntax and orthography of language are meddled with until the utterance reaches the brink of mean-inglessness; joke brand names like 'Kleen-E-Ze' or the extra-ordinary conflations one finds on tins of pet food do to language exactly what the *Kitsch*-manufacturing business does to the new synthetic plastics and metals. They play libidinous games with the kinds of social order and utility that are traditionally inherent in the material. Try following the grammar and vocabulary of this advertisement, taken from a copy of *TV Times*:

> Happy-go-lightly, colour. Wild, toe-happy Spring has come a-running! JOYCE HAPPIES—name of a shoe! Joyce have put colour into, fun into, fashion into Happies . . . and you won't even know they're on your feet. Happie ness starts at 59/11.

Unfortunately, it's difficult to quote ads in this sort of context without automatically sounding like a mournful liberal con-templating the fallen world of other people. What strikes me as interesting about this one is its resolute anarchism of tone; the way it uses a mixture of archaism, joke illiteracy, un-grammaticalness, and deliberately over-placed rhetorical devices to subvert any consistency of voice behind it. It is impossible to imagine a person speaking it (hard, for that matter, to imagine anyone writing it). It is a piece of language that has been carefully and cleverly stripped of its social dimensions, turned into an impersonal object. Yet, a few pages later in the same issue of *TV Times*, one comes across an advertisement which seems positively clogged with intimate social undertones:

> We don't want you feeding your car the wrong oil.
>   It's all very nice saving money by doing
> your own topping-up and oil changing.
>   But it's important to choose the right oil
> at the right price.
>   So, to help you choose right, we'll tell
> you which Esso oil does what.

Esso's lugubriously bedside manner works ultimately to the same effect as Joyce's happie anarchism; it liberates *parole* from its social connexions by demonstrating that they can be played with, irrespective of the actual social context. In such a situation *parole* has become subject to so many vagaries, a plastic tissue at the mercy of the professional communicator's whim, that it ceases to be socially manageable; we are left confronting the empty infinities of the *langue*.

This, I think, is a fair, if diagrammatic, model of what has happened to whole areas of language in contemporary culture; though it's important to add that it is distinctly unhelpful to retreat into the customary moans about the 'debasement of language'. Rather, one needs to acknowledge that industrial means of transmission (beginning, inevitably, with Gutenberg and Caxton, but accelerating with real effect only since the 1880s, with the rise of the mass-circulation popular newspaper and the emergence of the characteristic *Tit-Bits* style) have radically changed the social premises on which we believe language to be dependent. Our sense of context, of the underlying certainties of grammar and tone, has been undermined; we have, in precise Marxian terms, become alienated from our language. The markedly twentieth-century sensitivity to cliché is a major symptom of our condition; we have acquired an easy suspicion of linguistic forms, a tendency to relegate every utterance to some discredited context where it may be seen as 'jargon'. Edward Dorn, in his long, discursive poem 'Oxford', voices a disillusion which is itself a peculiarly contemporary kind of cliché:

> We have had race
> and color and oppression/oppressor
> shoved up our asses so long
> we don't even see that, *even poets*
>   are no longer in communication.
> Yevtushenko talking like the chamber of commerce
> in Washington
> inside the same general language

it is that *bad*, "the many languages
of English"
are as if
they were "foreign", as if commodity
had turned all that sound off, and into
the international times.

Indeed, camp wit, which in London and New York at any rate, is the form of speech which currently passes most easily for intelligence, is a style of deliberate cliché; it exploits the 'foreignness' of language by turning everything into a series of tongue-in-cheek platitudes. One can only speak freely by loftily dissociating oneself from what one says; as if the language had died, and its users had been left playing with its dry bones like larking morticians. Every available style becomes a piece of period junk, good for a sophisticated, supercilious giggle.

But this is very much more than a smart, passing fad; it registers one of the deepest of all twentieth-century responses to language—the conviction that one's own identity is in question when one adopts a verbal form, that one may be merely a kind of robot, shuffling through a programmed circuit fed into one by the media who own and control the language. The entire system of relationships by which sentences are formed—the rhetoric and grammar—has become suspect; we are left with *words* alone, severed from their contexts, disembodied, free-floating. When Roland Barthes, in *Writing Degree Zero*, attempts a definition of the break between 'classical' (in his terms, pre-1848) and 'modern' poetry he centres it upon the distinction between a rhetoric of relationships and a series of unconnected signs:

Modern poetry, since it must be distinguished from classical poetry and from any type of prose, destroys the spontaneously functional nature of language, and leaves standing only its lexical basis. It retains only the outward shape of relationships, their music, but not their reality. The Word shines forth above a line of relationships emptied of their content, grammar is bereft of its purpose, it becomes prosody and is no longer anything but an inflexion which lasts only to present the Word.

If both my own and Barthes's statements sound so generalized as to be pieces of fringe metaphysics, they find a startlingly concrete correlative in William Burroughs's apologia for 'Cut ups':

> Cut ups are for everyone. Any body can make cut ups. It is experimental in the sense of being *something to do*. Right here write now . . . Cut the words and see how they fall. Shakespeare and Rimbaud live in their words. Cut the word lines and you will hear their voices. Cut ups often come through as code messages with special meaning for the cutter. Table tapping? Perhaps. Certainly an improvement on the usual deplorable performance of contacting poets through a medium. Rimbaud announces himself to be followed by some excruciatingly bad poetry. Cutting Rimbaud's words and you are sure of good poetry at least . . .

Of course, this extraordinary assumption only follows if you are prepared to agree that a desocialized language, stripped of its syntax, its means of making relationships between words, its systems of order, can still retain its power to mean and move. Or, putting it another way, grammar belongs to society, and can be ditched, while words are the property of the poet and are unpolluted. (It's worth noting, in passing, that Burroughs and Brion Gysin, friends and collaborators, seem to disagree, with important consequences, over whether the writer 'owns' his words. According to Burroughs, anyone can cut up Rimbaud, but the quality-guarantee of the result still appears to be vested in the original authorship of the poem.) So the disaffection with 'language' expresses itself in the icon-worship of 'words'.

'Words', in fact, come to constitute a Platonic overworld, a 'lexical playfield'—in Nabokov's phrase, borrowed by Tony Tanner as a chapter heading for his *City of Words*—into which the components of language can be temporarily liberated, given games to play, or toys to make. This happens most explicitly in the work of those American pop painters and designers who use graphics as the primary elements of their collages. The poem-paintings of Al Hansen, for instance, endlessly redistribute the words found on Hershey Bar wrappers, discovering all sorts of hidden erotic messages in a language that can, quite literally, be found blowing down every gutter on every street-corner in the United States. This enterprise has a flavour of almost Wordsworthian earnestness about it; betraying a romantic, missionary endeavour to go out into society's most ordinary and dreary corners in order to retrieve concealed truths and save them for Art. So the most 'corrupt' or 'debased' language—of advertising, politics, or suburban cliché—serves as a *langue* from which the poet can quarry a new *parole* of individual words, cut up, rearranged and dignified by its ten-dollar hard-bound or art-gallery context.

But if one looks at Hansen's collages, what is most immediately striking about them is the way each word still carries vestigial traces and scars of its original context; the Hershey Bar wrapper continues to stay very much in evidence, however much Hansen displaces its individual features. There is a real tension (and this is characteristic of Burroughs's cut-ups too) between the impulse towards change and re-creation and the essential intractability, the objective weight, of the linguistic material. 'Language' has come to perform a very similar function to that of the 'social world' of the realist novel; it is credited with having a concrete existence *out there*, with releasing a current of resistance against which the writer carries out a series of tentative negotiations. It's important to see that this effect is a self-fulfilling prophecy, or fiction; words don't, of necessity, retain their contexts, unless the writer/rearranger chooses to make them do so. I think it's best to see concrete poetry and the cut-up as variations of realism; the distinction they exert between 'art' and 'life', between the autonomous structure of the poem and the objective world which supplies its components, is a very familiar one indeed. So too are the puritanical moral overtones of conversion and rescue. What is new is the reductive paring down of the elements of realism to the opposition between 'language' and 'words'; a shrinkage that follows on, quite logically, from the aesthetics of Zola and Flaubert.

Concrete poetry entails a radical revaluation of the role and identity of the poet. The stylist, the inventor and controller of language, goes out, and in his place comes a new figure; an indifferent observer, a games-player and toy-maker, whose impersonal experiments often try to echo the mechanical processes of the binary computer. Prufrock's self-mocking question 'Do I dare disturb the universe?' gets adopted as a slogan to adorn a policy of non-interference. When the poem as a form interrogates the world its line of inquiry is not, as it was for the Romantics, 'what is in me?', but 'what is in the words that make up the world we live in?' The joke, the game, the audacious permutation, become means of exploring the objective domain of words and sentences. Edwin Morgan, to my mind one of the most interesting of the concretists, has a poem called 'Seven Headlines', based on a single line from Rimbaud's *Une Saison en Enfer*, 'Il faut être absolument moderne'. (See opposite page.)

This is a game in which language is reduced to a set of rules as precise as those of chess. Not only does Morgan strictly adhere to the original sequence of letters in Rimbaud's line, but he limits himself to finding only sentences which conform to the syntactical shape of the newspaper headlines (OLD SOLEMN ODE SOLD FOR FENDER IRON/ BOLD TREND IN LETTER TO SOLO READER/ ARSON IN BOLT FROM BLUE/ ABSENT FOOD BUD FOUND/ UTTER FERMENT IN REASON/ TEAM FEED AT MODERN LODE/ NO FETTER FOR ABSOLUTE MODERN MEN). As with all games, the rules announce themselves by their arbitrariness, and an essential feature of Morgan's poem is the way it suggests all sorts of other,

```
                    ol          d
                    sol    e    m      n
                    o              de
                    sol         d
          f                o              r
          f    e                n     der
i              r      o                        n
                    b ol         d
            tre              n    d
i                            n
      l    et                    t      er
                            t    o
                    sol           o
            re a                    der
      a    r   so    n
i                                        n
                    b ol    t
          f   r    o    m
                    b  lu  e
        a        bs   ent
          f            o          od
                    b   u          d
          f          o  u    n      d
      ut t e                          r
          f    e r          ment
i                            n
            re a so      n
            t e a        m
          f    e e                  d
        a t                    modern
                        l          ode
                            n    o
          f    et                t      er
          f              o              r
                    absolu     t     e
                        m    odern
                        men
il faut être absolument moderne
```

equally arbitrary, possibilities. If you choose to find other 'messages' in the line you can permutate them beside Morgan's chosen examples:

> It fares us ill, it's solemn treason
> To let our fabled lease on reason
> Falter,
>
>   For our rent is a mere nod
> To our Realtor . . .

—for instance, borrowing a rather more archaic convention than that of the newspaper headline. As Brion Gysin indicates in the quotation at the head of this chapter, the permutated poem symbolizes, in part at least, the way in which language can cease to be a personal commodity, owned by the poet. The concretist vests his authority as a writer in his access to *means* and *services*; in structures and techniques which can be used to generate poems, but which lay no exclusive, personalist claim to 'the best words in the best order'. I think there's a useful analogy here with avant-garde movie-making (especially Andy Warhol and his disciples), where the camera is used as a mechanical intermediary between the artist and the object in front of his lens. Its technical openings and limitations, of light, angle of view, and focus, are incorporated into the presentation of the film; they become part of the objective nature of what lies in front of the movie-maker. For the concretists the poem is frequently treated like a camera; a kind of gadget which will formulate rules and patterns almost independent of the person of the poet. The writer is there to set the stops and oil the mechanism, but the real work of making the poem is seen to take place in the functioning of the language itself. So Emmett Williams has a poem in which the three words 'like attracts like' are arranged in converging columns until they eventually merge with one another in an overprint: 'likeacks'. Williams comments: 'This particular poem says what it does, and does what it says'. The reasons for its shape and order inhere in the words themselves.

Alternatively, letters alone, set loose from their functions in words or sentences, may be allowed to form entirely abstract patterns. In this 'typestract' by Dom Sylvester Houédard the medium of the poem isn't language at all, but its mechanical means of reproduction, in the technical resources of the typewriter. Here the word 'atom' has been so literally atomized that its original semantic value becomes a relatively trivial component in the larger play of meaning

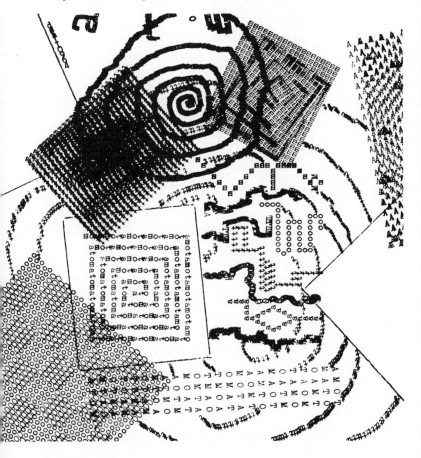

between lines, squiggles, curves, and rectangles. Indeed, the nonsense words into which 'atom' is anagrammatized in the long rectangle at the bottom of the composition are made just as 'meaningful' in the local terms of the typestract as the 'real' word from which they're made.

```
a     a     a     a     a
   c     c     c     c
r     r     r     r     r
   o     o     o     o
b     b     b     b     b
   a     a     a     a
t     t     t     t     t
   s     s     s     s
t     t     t     t     t
   a     a     a     a
b     b     b     b     b
   o     o     o     o
r     r     r     r     r
   c     c     c     c
a     a     a     a     a
```

In Ian Hamilton Finlay's 'Acrobat' the letters of the word are made to perform stunts; and Finlay designed this poem to occupy a whole wall of a children's playground in giant characters, so that the letters themselves would become toys in their comically exaggerated scale.

Again we're curiously close to Wordsworth here—in particular, to the final stanzas of 'The Idiot Boy', with their artfully innocent attempt to subvert, or make literal, the accustomed conventions of language:

> Now Johnny all night long had heard
> The owls in tuneful concert strive;
> No doubt too he the moon had seen;
> For in the moonlight he had been
> From eight o'clock till five.
>
> And thus, to Betty's question, he
> Made answer, like a traveller bold,
> (His very words I give to you,)
> 'The cocks did crow to-whoo, to-whoo,
> And the sun did shine so cold!'
> —Thus answered Johnny in his glory
> And that was all his travel's story.

For both Wordsworth and Finlay the figure of the child is central as a kind of hypothetical mode of perception, because the child is able to apprehend language as *words*; manipulable counters in a prelapsarian Eden which hasn't yet become staled and codified by conventional usage. Johnny's couplet is virtually a concrete poem; just as Finlay makes idiot children of us all, if we are to successfully enter the toy world of his poem. Though one needs to add that Wordsworth's and Finlay's versions of 'innocence' are equally conventional and diagrammatic; they are postulations about a way in which we might, but almost invariably can't, respond to language.

Yet, in a sense, the twentieth-century poet does—unlike Wordsworth—live in a world where *words*, shorn of the conventions of syntax, are able to work like magical, talismanic icons. Like the internationalism of the concretists (who correspond between Asia and Central Europe, Scotland, Australia, the United States, and South America), the trans-geographical frontiers of the counter-culture are maintained by a system of words which are exchanged as signals, told like beads. There exists a single code, compounded of a vocabulary drawn from black slang, the argots of jazz, drugs, and folk-psychoanalysis. Like all codes, it reinforces the boundaries of the community; keeping outsiders out, insiders in. The sentence concertinas down to the single word: 'score', 'high', 'flip-out', 'freaky', 'bust', and so on. Mental states are compressed into isolated, powerful metaphors: 'uptight', 'hang-up', 'mind-fuck'. Hippie conversation possesses an extraordinary asyntacticality; all the usual structures of explanation and qualification tend to get subsumed under the universal expressions 'like' and 'right'. The word 'right', in fact, which has a habit of recurring monotonously as both interrogation and emphasis (Right? . . . Right!), is a typical signaller's code device, indicating 'Message understood'. In consonance with this deliberate avoidance of grammar, of the despised societal relationships (and the rational systems) which are implicit in the syntax of language, the celebrative rituals of the counter-culture focus on the incantation of disjunctive (and, I suspect, for all practical purposes, meaningless) word-phrases like the *Hare Krishna*. As I write (February 1971), the top of the British Top Ten is George Harrison's 'My Sweet Lord', a repetitive dirge in which Harrison drones out the words of the title along with the lines 'I really want to be with you' and 'Hare Krishna'. Indeed, the Beatles' development, if that's the term, from the whimsical intricacies of the early Lennon-McCartney lyrics to the latest of the Lennon-Ono and Harrison chanted slogans, has been symptomatic of the accelerating revolt against syntax and the corresponding mystical infatuation with the Word. Predictably enough, Jackson Mac Low has written a concrete poem called '4th Hare Krsna Gatha' in which 'HARE KRSNA' and 'RAMA' are

permutated in block letters of varying sizes over a sheet of
squared paper; the empty squares stand, we're told, for both
space and time, and if you really want to you can chant it,
playing music or other non-verbal sounds to fill up the spaces
between the letters and words.

There is, in all this, a fairly impenetrable mixture of
solemnity, silliness, and amusing games and tricks. If one
flicks through an anthology of concrete poetry one can't help
being struck by the puritanical air of righteous minimalism.
It is as if these prettily arranged slogans, slender jokes, and
elegant examples of the craft of the typographer were the
very last unpolluted goods that could be salvaged from the
ruins of a corrupted language. They stand in relation to the
central body of contemporary English and American poetry
much as the sacking-and-scrubbed-deal Health Food restaurant does to the steak house. They self-consciously ex-
emplify the virtues of impoverishment and deprivation. The
image of the child, and the childish game, becomes substituted
for the compromised figure of the adult negotiating with his
language as a web of relationships. The concrete poem is the
product of a tribal and ritualistic culture—a kind of culture
which the English or American writer in the twentieth
century can only effectively inhabit as a dream. The internationalism of concrete verse, along with its totemic worship
of words and its construction of tiny, utopian play-universes,
makes it a form of para-poetry; it operates most satisfactorily
as a wing of literary criticism.

At the same time, concrete poetry is perhaps the most
violent (in its puritan fashion) expression of a widespread,
often unfocused and illogical, belief that language, in its more
complex relations, has been irretrievably *dirtied*. These
images of cleanliness and pollution are important. As Mary
Douglas has shown in her two books, *Purity and Danger* and
Natural Symbols, our assumptions about culture and language,
about 'truth' and 'goodness', are deeply rooted in the way in
which we manage and think about our bodies. The notion of

the befouled language, and its possible rehabilitation through breaking it down into its constituent parts, needs to be set beside the current ecological craze with its emphasis on the pollution of both the natural environment and society. Mary Douglas implies that we are all a little purity-and-pollution mad at present (a characteristic of a society anxiously defining its own changing boundaries); concrete poetry, the macrobiotics of the literary world, could provide her with a good deal of evidence to support her argument. It is, at least, a major symptom of the kind of weather in which poems are now being written.

Indeed, concrete verse, along with the diffidently minimal almost-poems of a British writer like Hugo Williams and the broken, shortlined, It-is-practically-impossible-to-say-any-thing-at-all poems of Robert Creeley, is primarily important for the way in which it stakes out the edge of the desert, beyond which no poetry can be written at all. The joke, the silence, and the word-picture sit on the margin of contemporary verse; significantly and continuously visible, like warning notices. My own feeling is that those writers who have espoused them as forms sufficient in themselves are practising a kind of exemplary necromancy; fascinated by the violence or starvation which it is possible to inflict on a poem and its language before it eventually expires, turns into a bad pun, or becomes a painting. But these experiments, products of a climate in which we have learned to subject our own language to an intense, alienated scrutiny, have given a special resonance to other, more traditional and central, attempts to sustain a full and flexible social voice in the poem. A lot of the recent, argumentative energy of the work of British writers like Alan Brownjohn and Donald Davie (a relatively new feature in their verse) does seem to stem from a conscious, often angry, sometimes bitterly ironical, dialectical rejection of the concrete-and-minimalist avant-garde. A couple of years ago, when *The Times Literary Supplement* published a concrete poem by Edwin Morgan, a literary row ensued that trailed through the correspondence columns for weeks.

For the concrete poem dramatizes an aesthetic. It poses a theory of art as play, of verse as a sort of verbal nursery or *Spielraum*. It rejects language as it is used in the muddied moral and commercial waters of society, except in so far as it provides a patient, ripe for rehabilitation by play-therapy. It turns poems into public objects, toys divorced from the personal voice and authorship of their constructor. It looks more to the abstract expressionist painters than to literary traditions for its formal models. It works in glancing, instantaneous effects; its rhythms belong more to the quick-fire pace of the television image or the billboard passed at speed in a railway carriage than they do to the reflective, recurrent metrical patterns of conventional poetry. It is a truly technological art, depending on the typewriter or letterpress, and the point at which concrete poetry becomes distinctively separate from the graphics industry is an extremely ambiguous one. As long ago as 1898 Arthur Symons in his essay on Beardsley pointed out that the ballet, the circus, and the music-hall were major sources for contemporary painting (especially for Degas, Lautrec, and Beardsley), because their rapid, elliptical effects provided concrete analogies to the constantly moving, fleeting visual experiences of the inhabitant of the industrial city. 'Modern' art was essentially the art of the poster. Symons's statement holds well for concrete poetry; except that we shouldn't be misled into a simple-minded determinism of the kind which dictates that the truest art is the one which runs most freely into the bondage of local social, technological, and industrial circumstances.

7

Talking Heads

> And Landor, Pound and Browning are
> All in this sense too insular
> To help us much, who need to probe
> A way to humanise the globe
>
> DONALD DAVIE, 'Fourth Epistle
to Eva Hesse'

If language sometimes seems to have rotted away, exposing its bare skeleton of words, and if the means of communication seem to have retreated beyond the reach of the individual—to have become impersonal, technologized—it has become an act of some daring to speak at all. Yet it's increasingly true that what we as a society, a *public*, are asking of the poet is that he provide us with 'a voice'. One of the striking things about attending a poetry reading is the way in which its audience seems to cluster, like a gathering of devout early Christians, in the hope of hearing a private language spoken in public. Often it isn't the flamboyantly entertaining, performed poems which go down best at a reading, but those poems which talk from the intimacy of a private experience. When a man talks about fearing his own death, or witnessing the birth of his child, or recounts the progress of a failed love affair to a filled auditorium, one can frequently sense the *frisson* of gratification amongst the audience; this is what they have needed, this is what they have come to hear. It is as if the poet had appropriated the role of the old-style country parson or family doctor; a man whose expertise lies in his capacity for immediate intimacy. Just recently the Greater London Arts Association have started a dial-a-poem service (01-836-2872); interestingly, the poems chosen to be recorded by the writers themselves have tended to be private, confessional,

soft-voiced. It's not unlike being able to dial your own anonymous caller, complete with heavy breathing. The real service
provided is a *voice*; gentle and intimate words for anyone who
has the price of a phone call. Publishers have instinctively
recognized this; there has been a notable, even obsessional,
recurrence of the word 'voice' in the titles of post-war collections and anthologies—*Voices, New Voices, The Poet's
Voice*, and so on.

The poet's peculiar relationship with the language of
society has made him the object of a nostalgic myth amongst
his public; we tend to expect, as of right, to inhabit an intimate community in the language of the poem. And the ex-
pectation has become more insistent as society at large has
moved more inextricably into the relatively impersonal en-
vironments of the big city and the corporation. The sweet-
and-weepy verses which act as fillers in the corners of British
women's weeklies, and the massive sales enjoyed by Mary
Wilson's book of amateur, housewifely poems (sales which
are only partially accounted for by the behind-the-parlour-
door-at-Number-Ten aspect of the volume), are expressions
of a naïve but strongly held belief in the idea of the poet as
custodian of private values, a person who can speak directly,
independent of the media, of expert jargons, of all the aliena-
tive forces which keep us apart from our language. The poet
gets romantically valued as a survivor from some pre-industrial Eden.

What is most interesting about this is the way it simultaneously supports and conflicts with the tradition of dramatic monologue which the contemporary poet has inherited
through Browning, Eliot, and Pound. From Fra Lippo Lippi
and Andrea del Sarto to Pound's Personae—his resurrected
Chinese mandarins and Provençal troubadours, along with
the Janus-like rhetorical sage who sits at the centre of the
Cantos—modern poetry (and the statement is equally true of
the modern novel; one thinks especially of recent writers like
Saul Bellow and Philip Roth) is haunted by monologists.

Indeed, as Robert Langbaum has helped to show in *The Poetry of Experience*, the dramatic monologue is *the* modern verse form; as a style it enables the world to report back to, and inform, the poem. The person of the speaker becomes a device for embodying the extreme, or outrageous, or paradoxical moral attitude; the constant tension between the swaggering energy of his own voice and the containing shape of the poem makes for a continuing dialogue between the profuse, muddled pluralism of experience and the ordered, rhythmic design of art. But monologue as a form cannot bear too much instability; it depends for its existence on a world of 'characters', where the human identity at the centre of the poem, however bizarre or distorted, is certain; where a voice can go on talking without interruption. For Pound, as for Browning, the monologue is rooted in a basic confidence—in society, or at least its 'saving remnant' and its shared consensus of values, in social language and its expressive deviations, and in an essentially nineteenth-century, novelistic notion of character.

In our own time so much has changed that we have been left with the mere technical husk of the dramatic monologue; conventions for creating a speaking human voice without the web of metaphysical assurances which brought them into being. Contemporary verse is full of talkers, but they have a lonely, worried, timorously assertive air; they are the voice on the telephone which expects to be cut off at any moment, the voice of a passing stranger in a rush-hour subway, or the voice of the prophet who has to create his own, utopian universe in order to speak at all.

Leaving for a while the more complicated case of those writers who are negotiating and compromising with the full force of literary tradition, as well with immediate social circumstances (like Davie, Porter, Brownjohn, Larkin, Lowell, Snodgrass), let us look at the extreme solutions posed by some of the younger English and American poets who, through regional groups and poetry readings, have been most directly involved in this problem of finding a speaking voice for the poem. In San Francisco, and Liverpool, and Newcastle upon Tyne, there was a steady movement during the 1960s towards a style of whimsically impoverished speech, an attempt to get a local, private, dispossessed language into verse, to talk straight, bypassing poetic convention, to the audience. It is a curiously bastardized style; owing something to the ad-libbed backchat of the stand-up comic, something to the language of movie dialogue, where the giant projected face is able to talk in a quick-fire undertone to the world at large, and something to the mesmeric relationship between the pop singer and his public.

What, for instance, does one make of this, the first stanza of a poem by Roger McGough, called 'Aren't We All':

Looks quite pretty lying there
Can't be asleep yet
Wonder what she's thinking about?
Penny for her thoughts
Probably not worth it.
There's the moon trying to look romantic
Moon's too old that's her trouble
Aren't we all?

Here is a voice which seems to have shambled, almost unawares, with a kind of coy cool, into 'poetry'. I think the main pleasure in listening to this poem, when McGough performs it, is that of seeing an official world of Elizabethan love lyrics and their popular derivatives, complete with moons and sleeping girls and insomniac lovers, invaded by the young man from next door. An obvious, but often missed, feature of the work of all the Liverpool poets in their dependence on conventions which are sufficiently overused to have become public clichés; they are almost invariably engaged in writing thumb-nose footnotes to the Love Poem, the Elegy, the Epithalamium, the Ode, the Nursery Rhyme, the Moral Tale. It's a Chaplinesque occupation, involving a raggy insolence towards the institution of poetry.

The voice it produces is one of comically straight-faced, down-at-heel realism; flat, wry, debunking in the style of an old, Come-Off-It-Mate *Daily Mirror* editorial. McGough's poems, particularly, reduce down to a series of puns and epigrams:

> you will put on a dress of guilt
> and shoes with broken high ideals . . .
> Or when I'm 91
> with silver hair
> & sitting in a barber's chair
> may rival gangsters
> with hamfisted tommyguns burst in
> & give me a short back & insides

Such small, quixotic jokes stake out the boundary between the cosy conversational humour of the ordinary world of the poem and the untrustworthy territory beyond, where the high rhetoric of love and death and disease begins. ('When I'm 73/& in constant good tumour') But if we listen to the undertone of these poems there is an alarming note of self-congratulation about the tiny, whimsical community in which they allow their audience to nestle; a cocky, Keep-On-Smiling, Don't-Let-Life-Get-You-Down philistinism. One of the preoccupations shared by Adrian Henri, Roger McGough, Brian Patten, and Henry Graham is a tedious sentimentality directed variously at small children and pubic schoolgirls. It's appropriate enough; for the communal voice of their poetry speaks, with Salinger's Holden Caulfield in *The Catcher in the Rye*, of the dreary disaster of having to grow beyond the age of fourteen. It invites us to return to the safe nursery-world of gym-slips and fish-and-chips, of atrocious adolescent witticisms and the sort of arch knowingness that passes, at that age, for world-weary cynicism. Henry Graham has a poem called 'Sociosexual primer for children of all ages' which rehearses jokey definitions of 'Womb', 'Birth', 'Mother', 'Father', 'Puberty', 'Intercourse', 'Love', and ends with a blank space under the heading 'Marriage'; you can almost hear the giggle at that point, as the voice stops, facetiously within its limits.

Yet this determined childishness, the sustained *faux naïf* pose, does release a speaking voice which is able to talk freely from inside its retardations. It announces itself, as do so many of these puritan, minimalist styles of contemporary verse, as the nearest thing to an honest voice that we have in a society of corrupted and compromised adults. At the same time it has corruptions of its own; beneath the wide-eyed chatter of flowers and nymphets there lurks a corresponding insensitivity, the totalitarian toughness of the playground bully, the taunting voice of the smart-alecky child who is baiting Teacher. In 'Schoolboy', by Brian Patten, we are invited to attend an updated lesson on the shades-of-the-prison-house-close-in theme by Wordsworth. Patten celebrates his child with a whimsical innocence he has borrowed from E. E. Cummings (by far the most important 'influence' on the Liverpool poets):

> The schoolyard's full of people to hate.
> Full of tick and prefects and a fat schoolmaster
> and whistles and older and younger boys, but
> he's growing
>   sadly
>   growing
>   up.

But this is a voice which can only achieve a dubious articulacy when its narrowed terms are directed abusively against the world outside the playground. Patten soon loses his charm when he contemplates, for instance, the headmaster:

> The headmaster's crying in his study.
> His old pinstriped pants rolled up to his knees
> in a vain attempt to recapture youth; emotions
> skid along his slippery age; Love, smeared across his face,
> like a road accident.

This is a hugely recognizable style in what I feel is the worst of contemporary verse. The words ooze with relish at their power to hurt, or insult, or condescend; a power which they have earned by a process of rigid exclusion, a rhetorical narrowing down to a child's, or an ideologue's, or a worm's-eye view.

One catches exactly the same note in some of the political poems of Adrian Mitchell and Alan Bold, or, on a grander scale, in the capitalized outbursts of Michael McClure and Leroi Jones. A voice is justified on the righteous grounds that we need to salvage some stable, human vantage-point from which to make sense of the confusions of society and its language; it is then used to create a purblind, monocular dictatorship within the poem. The child, the black, the man of conscience, the aggressive provincial become devices for generating rhythms, epithets, and metaphors whose force stems from their narrowness; you can, after all, produce a fiercer and more strident sound from a bugle than from a bassoon.

It is, indeed, the very opposite of what Browning was doing in his monologues; the style of the human voice has become a means not of inclusion but of exclusion—a way, not of getting the world in, but of commanding a very small, eccentric position on it which will throw its complexities into an exaggeratedly distant perspective. Two brief quotations here, from poems by Adrian Mitchell:

> After the next war . . . and the sky
> Heaves with contaminated rain.
> End to end our bodies lie.
> Round the world and back again.

> Observe that man and see the lust
> Bulging his serge as he cons a bust.
> If he had to go cannibal he would eat
> Only blonde secretarial meat.
> His wife and his house and his brain are dim.
> He didn't invent sex. Sex invented him.

One only has to remember Pope's *Dunciad* to think of a style which turns society into a raw material which can be processed into brilliant, sharp, transcendent metaphors. But what is going on here is rather different. The metaphors themselves are contemptuously facile, throwaway. Mitchell seems to be entranced with the kind of verbal symmetry one can get with a deliberately cheap and flashy generalization, the gutter proverb. Quite unlike an Augustan satirist, he gives us nothing to pause over; the metre trills regularly along, pulling the reader at a hectic speed over the easy hyperboles and sour quips that go on in the language of the poem. What one responds to is not the activity of the verse so much as the tone in which it's delivered; the only thing human left after a Mitchell poem has done its work is the rasping voice of the poet himself. It is like being challenged to gaze back into a long, righteous sneer. At poetry readings, where he is an accomplished performer, Mitchell often appears to be re-creating the role of Olivier's Richard III; a hunched, snapping figure, who has the power to divide his audience into two factions. Either you adopt the persona of the poem or you become its fall-guy victim, the object of its disgust. And just as Roger McGough uses literary conventions as pegs on which to pin his voice, so Mitchell uses social and political ones; he hangs his poems on issues like Vietnam, the Royal Family, the Conservative Party, the ostrich-Poujadism of the lower-middle class, the nuclear-arms race—polarizing topics where our loyalties are already staked out, and the poem can afford merely to fuel and inflame them.

Such voices demand that we respond first and foremost to their charisma; their strategy is one of total statement which will brook no argument. (How different, again, from the end-less self-justifications of the men and women who talk in the poetry of Browning and Pound.) The obscenity and the slogan become zeniths, towards which the poem must inevitably mount; for anything less is likely to smack of the despised liberal consensus with its passion for all-inclusive, all-amiable rationality. So Michael McClure's verse is strung out between capitalized headlines, summary slogans which command total assent before you can proceed to the rest of the poem in small type:

OH I AM BLIND AS A FLOWER AND SENSE LESS
    we see nothing but banality.
Break in the forms and take real postures!

This is the real world clear and open.
The flower moves and motion is its sense,
    and transference of ions
    all that it does is perception
        and vision.
OH BREAK UP THE POEMS AND FEEL NEW THINGS

If we find McClure's slogans banal to the point of being ludicrous, that, presumably, is all to the good. The Voice has spoken, and it is up to the reader only to take sides. More recently ('The Flowers of Politics', from which my quotation is taken, was written in 1959) McClure has moved in decisively on the world of sex, and his current poems tend to use the words 'FUCK!!' and 'SHIT!!' (his ejaculation marks) to sort out the sheep from the goats among us.

McClure uses a particular vocal style to enforce ritual boundaries; either the reader becomes one of the faithful or else he is excluded, as a cynical onlooker, from the society of the poem. But the act of faith is made before the poem begins; if you don't happen to share the language, McClure won't condescend to talk you into being converted. It's exactly the same ploy as Michael Horovitz uses in his 'Afterwords' to *The Children of Albion* anthology of British Underground verse; where he erects a slangy, pseudo-Blakean 'cornucopia' to contain the wilted flowers and bruised fruits of his collection. Rather than working as a commentary on the poems, Horovitz's piece acts as a sheet of litmus paper on which to test his readers' sensibilities. Like the jargon of the New Left, this kind of style functions, not through the expressiveness of what it says, but as a flag waved on the front line; it incenses the enemy and acts as a rallying-point around which the armies of the faithful may gather.

The monologue (or, more accurately, the voiced poem which hinges on its local social tone) has recently been taken up more and more as a boundary-making form; a style which can correspond to the special privacy of modern social experience. It has become appropriated as the voice of the eccentric, or the revolutionary, or the threatened community. Its exclusions fend off the outside world, while what is included is hoarded preciously as the property of those readers who, with the writer, become insiders. Such a stance entails a delicate balancing act; and too many of these poems seem to concentrate themselves solely into a kind of hedgehog ball of spines—prickly and impenetrable unless you happen to be the hedgehog yourself. The most interesting exceptions seem to me to be the Newcastle poets who have grouped themselves round Basil Bunting (and through him have absorbed much of the spirit of Poundian modernism) and who've developed their voices, and the relationship between the written and the spoken poem, in verse-readings at the Morden Tower. On the surface, perhaps, nothing could look more exclusive and parochial than one's initial glimpse of a dialect poem by Tom Pickard; thus the first few lines of 'Shag':

> canny bord ower there
> sharrap man yi think i nowt but tarts
>
> divin na though
> wouden mind a bash arrit
>
> hoo pet can a tek yi yem?
> am a big streng lad
> al luk after yi
>
> a na ya not owld inuff ti suck a dummy
>
> hoo lads tommys scored
> whats ya name pet
> howear gis a kiss
> gis a bit feel pet . . .

Yet here the Geordie voice protects and nurses the experience that is happening in the lines of the poem. The transliteration of the accent is beautifully done, and Pickard has orchestrated the irregular, harsh rhythms of local speech in a way that is reminiscent of, and compares well with, William Carlos Williams. The group of lads and the prostitute become a containing, sufficient society within the poem; the extra-ordinary mixture of violence and tenderness enfolds the reader in a world which, amazingly, considering its apparent impoverishment of language, turns out to be big enough to live in. Pickard works with ballads, folksongs, street-corner dialogues, discovering a kind of emotional purity of expression among the voices to be heard in the backwaters of an indus-trial city. When he is not writing in dialect the language he uses has a hard-won simplicity; as if each phrase had been carefully retrieved and weighed for its metrical density. One can see in these poems the level of expressiveness to which the Geordie voices of his dialogues are aspiring; a sort of highly stylized version of 'the language used by men' which Wordsworth first explored in the *Lyrical Ballads*:

> warm folk say gudneet
>   drunk and huddled together
> their voices part on the river
>   soft hair warm breath
>   my hands on your breasts
>   your dress unzips
>   drunk and huddled together
>   bare by the river together
>   lap   lap lap
>   huddled together

Hovering just behind the lines of Pickard's work is a pro-tective nostalgia for a style of life that will correspond to the refined simplicities of his language; it is, I think, a weakening force, only a nudge or two away from a sentimental yearning for a lost 'organic' society. The voice he uses, in its rejection

of urban sprawl and complexity, slips too easily into a cosy
disgust, a chauvinistic, Little Newcastleism. The last stanza
of a poem about Soho, for instance:

> Pull your eyes from the windows
> and see where we are
> buying popcorn & arseholes
> icecream and baretits
> black flash of an overworked cunt
> anonymity
> to seek out our particular perversion
> white landrovers slither at the curb
> police inside observe

This strikes me as too whimsical a confrontation between
innocence and experience; the words fall too pat, the details
too predictably. In a sense it's a necessary poem for Pickard,
for it marks out the social frontier beyond which his verse
cannot go; but at the same time it betrays the reedy limitations of a voice which talks best when it stays firmly at home.
Newcastle and Soho are parts of an essentially symbolic
geography of the imagination; and Pickard's limp, alienated
glimpse of the metropolis corresponds to a boundary in his
poetry between the speakable and the merely describable.

Tom Raworth has, perhaps, come closest to making a style
of monologue which, though it protects the local, domestic
experience, does not stake out its frontier too close to the
perimeter of the home town. From a poem called 'You Were
Wearing Blue':

> i will wait at the station and you
> will send a note, i
> will read it
> it will be raining
>
> our shadows in the electric light
> when i was eight they taught me *real*
> writing
> to join up the letters

    listen you said i
    preferred to look
        at the sea. everything stops there at strange angles

This is a notation in which the voice circumscribes, makes footnotes to, a broken sequence of experience. Again, the spoken lines seem like 'retrievals'; they are the distilled residue of a pattern of life and conversation whose profusion and diversity is hinted at in the spaces and line-breaks which occupy so much of the poem. The lower-case 'i' sinks to the same, artfully undiscriminating-seeming level of the other people and things in the verse; a cipher which talks, but doesn't appear to control or impose its identity on what happens in the words. It is a first person that has been absorbed into the crowd of the poem; a voice which possesses only an accidental, circumstantial authority. Indeed—and this is characteristic of a great deal of recent poetry—it is rather as if one of the dispossessed people in the crowd of a nineteenth-century novel, or a twentieth-century newsreel, had been suddenly enfranchised, licensed to speak, not from a dominating, romantic notion of selfhood, but from a humble, unillusioned position in the ruck of a large community. The right to monologue has passed from Bishop Blougram to his almost invisible attendants. Prufrock has rid himself of the hysterical irony of his fallen, anti-heroic posture, and has, as it were, been reconciled to his station.

This transition has been much more painful and paradox-ridden (the apparent democratization of tone of the Liverpool poets and Adrian Mitchell swings, with alarming ease, as I've tried to show, into old-style authoritarianism in a new, demotic accent) for English writers than for Americans. Walt Whitman was, after all, singing in his bardic fashion of the joys of the *En Masse* more than a hundred years ago, and the tradition of monologue in American writing (its fiction as well as its poetry) has devolved on figures picked out from the crowd, from Ring Lardner's baseball players, through the patients in Dr Williams's general practice, to Salinger's bright, prep-school adolescents and the talking potheads of the West Coast scene. Writers from what is now getting known as 'The New York School', like Frank O'Hara and Kenneth Koch, are working on a style of rumbling, often verbose, monologue, in which the speaker of the poem is a kind of televisual talking head; verse turns into a metrically organized chat show, or a larynx movie.

But it's in the poetry of Edward Dorn that the tradition of monologue seems to me to be, for the time being, most fully sustained; of all recent writers Dorn has come nearest to making a voice that is natural, personal, and capable of speaking in a way that incorporates, rather than resists, the world outside the poem. *The North Atlantic Turbine*, his last-but-one collection, was a fine, swashbuckling raid on the genre of the spoken verse meditation; an attempt to salvage the relaxed, articulate individual voice for poetry. Dorn's speaking persona, which has gone through some sea-changes between the 1950s and the present, started with an all-too-recognizable appealing whimsy, a studied *simplesse*. His early poems are hardly more than verbal doodles, games played with the chance resources of language.

> Yi Yi, the cowboy's eyes
> are blue. The top of the sky
> is too.

is a characteristic, pretty strategy, from 'Vaquero' (1957). The poem is treated as a nursery full of entertaining toys— bad puns, tinkling rhymes, coy syntactical parallels, a collection of tricks for the voice to perform. Or a stanza from another poem written at the same time, 'The Hide of My Mother':

> Once my mother
> was making dinner
>
> and my cats were on the floor.
>
> Why do they whine like that?
> She asked,

why don't we throw them all out the door?
why don't you feed them I ventured?

She said she wasn't indentured.

Can you imagine telling a poet that?
Later she fed them my pet rat.

Compared with his friends Olson and Creeley, and the
messianic sonority of the Projective Verse programme, Dorn
at this stage seems like the spoiled baby brother of the Black
Mountaineers. The innocence of his speaking voice, as it
discovers itself in these fey simplicities, strikes one as appal-
lingly contrived. It is a voice which giggles fetchingly at its
own tiny jokes; a voice whose childishness is the sentimental
fabrication of an adult, like the over-indulged pranks of a
Dead End Kid or a Richmal Crompton William. But in retro-
spect one can see these poems as five-finger exercises for a
style in which the child's-eye view is beautifully and subtly
balanced (as it so lamentably fails to be in the poems of
McGough and Patten) against the weight of social and
political experience with which it comes to deal. Dorn's voice
works best over a long span, across which one can measure
its changes of tone and strategy, and feel the cumulative
pressure of its inventions (which are locally often slight);
indeed, the best way to read Dorn is to follow him speaking
his own poems on record. Here is a necessarily long quotation
from the title-poem of *The North Atlantic Turbine*:

            What must be destroyed is
      the present circus of the earth and
      the place to start is the North
      Atlantic turbulence
            English pound
                  swiss
                        banker
                              mini
                                    skirt

<pre>
          the american law
            of the nickel
              cigar,
                 or
                   How to Make
                     Trees
                       Out of
                         Sawdust,
                           w/howdy-do
                             you all
</pre>

or, as if to greet you w/   I'm from alabama
a vocabularial gesture of the middle finger   on every
known in some regions as 'the bird'   leaf
may I suggest we all change our present names
to J. P. Getty: we then all emigrate from Minnesota
w/ a million skins in our jeans, something to begin with.
and while we seem in our adventures to be merely
screwing the farmers' daughters we are
in 'reality' skimming the cream from the top
of her pail. 'Naturally' we 'eventually' tire
of the Vulgarity of the United Statesety and
Settle in London, until, again with a vocabularial
gesture, we 'admit' that, altho the Bunnies' thighs
are hot and Hugh Heffner thinks our gonads
are composed of solid philosophy, the fact is,
it is just too damned cold and our asses are freezing
in an 18th century manner. Dispirited at last,
and for good cause since our guests are more interested
in our money than in our philosophy, we install a pay phone
in the unheated Great Hall to stop their nicking
transatlantic conversations, and declare the immensely rich
(a term in our 'realism' we have come to use w/out
        embarrassment)
to be the most lonely of all peoples, whereupon
we empty the coins from the phone, grab a bunny by the tit
and split for Rome, find a largish pad on a hill
what won't flood, hang up 'our' paintings, throw
a party (Hello Dolly, Howdy do Tex, Barbara Madbutt there,
glad you all could come) and settle 'down'.

'Big *sy*stem! China-and-the-East
is simply an amateur West
in crude contradiction.
Any mass gadget can prolong,
as it adds to, world pain.
The equipment of the commodity-motivated killer is the
thing under your nose. Whitman carried
into the administration tower of the U. of Takes-us
    underarm spray deodorant. I
date the urgency as before reversions i.e.,
*auto*mobiles reach China.'

    End-O-China

This deceptively throwaway style strikes me as an astonishingly successful attempt at straight-talking monologue. On the one hand, it is a verse of ambitiously large statement: it explores the essentially Marxian notion of the way in which particular features of the superstructure—the small details of social life, cigars, deodorants, clothes, possessions—cohere around an economic and ideological base. The 'North Atlantic turbulence' becomes the hub of a capitalist system which finds only an inverted mirror in the communism of the Eastern world; while American expatriatism, the styles of the well-heeled drop-out and the jeaned radical, is discovered not as an escape from, but as integral part of, the system. Even on this level of crude summary it would be hard to find a contemporary poem which had, to put it at its least, the arrogance of Dorn's frontal assault on the reigning ideologies of our time. But it is all done with a marvellously quirky individuality; with a voice that refuses to be cowed by the ideas it tackles. The pun and the joke are turned into a functional style, a way of asserting the particular in the midst of the general. So the University of Texas gets transmuted into the U. of Takes-us, in an act of cheeky expropriation; Indo-China finds itself occupied by Dorn's private army, and made over to the pacific industry of being The End, fairy-tale fashion. Dorn's voice, casual, amiable, slangy, is best at proving how the coldest and most formal-seeming issue can still be made available to a private man talking. The way he manages his line-endings and the typographical arrangement of the poem is lovingly attentive to the resources of tone and tempo in the speaking voice.

My own feeling is that the language of *The North Atlantic Turbine* comes as close as it is possible to move to the public demand for a humanizing voice which will speak clearly from the centre of what often seems to be an increasingly impersonal universe. If the audience at the poetry reading are searching simply for a human being to talk directly to them, then Dorn is their man. Yet Dorn himself has, I think, sensed the poetic limitations of this style; the reduction of verse to chat, the tendency of the poem to peter out into the monologue of an entertaining pub-raconteur. His most recent book, *Gunslinger*, has moved decisively away from the genial meditations of *The North Atlantic Turbine*. It opens on a stage direction: 'The curtain might rise/ anywhere on a single speaker'. But the single speaker of his new poem turns out to be a mythologist, a conscious and deliberate fiction-maker who inhabits a world at least one and a half removes from the here-and-now. Gunslinger is a comic-epic hero; a grizzled old-timer borrowed from the Western movie. Along with a brothel-keeping madam, and a talking, pot-smoking horse called Claude Levi Strauss, Gunslinger hits the trail in search of, first, Howard Hughes, and then of Universe City—the mythic temples of money and learning. Throughout the poem there are parodic echoes of Eliot and Whitman, along with games, puzzles, and jokey sections of self-commentary. During the second book, on the road to Universe City, there is an elaborate, and very funny, diversion in which 'I' gets turned into a third person, on the analogy of 'I got there ahead of myself', so that we get lines like

There was the faintest semblance
of a smile on I's posthumous mouth.

The speaking voice is endlessly made to attend to itself with a kind of anarchic irony. Of Gunslinger, in the middle of a farcical sequence involving the horse tossing his saddle through the doors of the saloon, Dorn writes:

> his head is a spasm
> of presyntactic metalinguistic urgency
>
> What What What
> Where Where Where
> Who What Where
> What Where Who

The style of monologue has become supportable only when it is accompanied by this sort of dicing with language; a nervous, ironic game played out on the edge of the poem, which opens everything that is said to an overwhelming lexical question. Like the novels of John Barth, Dorn's most recent poems have moved into the vertiginous territory of the fiction of fiction; of a landscape where reality is situated only in the temporary style, the partial verbal gesture, the imaginative pattern of myth. The certainty of the individual voice has gone, to be replaced by a baroque dramatic structure of literary references, cinema mythology, American historical symbolism, and the continual twitching of a voice talking about itself talking. It's an extremely interesting development, and Dorn's progress underlines that basic question as to whether the lone voice, speaking *in propria persona*, can ever be a sufficient form, however anxious the audience for poetry may be to respond to it. The talking heads of contemporary verse may well, I suspect, turn out to look like so many insubstantial spooks; summoned by a society which needed them for its own therapeutic reasons—because they offered a version of individual identity, of a personal authenticity of experience, of a private life secure in the midst of public confusion. But the pressure of literary tradition, of the complex possibilities of the language and form of poetry, has seduced most of our better writers away from the tantalizing simplicities of the straight-talking monologue.

8

A Place Not Our Own

Sailing away from ourselves, we feel
The gentle tug of water at the quay—
Language of the liberal dead speaks
From the soil of Highgate, tears
Show a great water table is intact.
You cannot leave England, it turns
A planet majestically in the mind.

PETER PORTER, 'The Last of England'

The writers I was discussing in the last chapter all practise
(or have practised) a modish ideology of innocence. Children
and provincial naifs figure in their work as symbols of a state
of mind; a style of consciousness for which history offers no
useful precedents, and which receives all its experience in an
unfiltered blaze of sensation. Literature for them has to be
invented as if no literary form had ever existed before; as if
we had only voices in the street to go on, and the cumulative
experience of tradition amounted merely to a collection of
dusty files in the cellars of the academy. The rejection of the
cultural centre and the adoption of a childish, or provincial,
or eccentrically private voice have tended to make the poet
into a professional solipsist; they have given him an exaggerated sense of his own uniqueness and a kind of mechanical
radicalism of tone. An essential feature of all the monologues
I was looking at is their reductive syntactical simplicity; their
speakers scorn qualification and never lose themselves, like
Browning's muddled and self-justifying men and women, in
the interstices of their own sentences. For, in a world you
invent every time you start to speak again, there is nothing to
justify, no qualifications to be made, the new is always
incomparable, and the past is little more than the torn-off

leaves of an outdated calendar. At its deepest this intuition has given a resonantly lonely quality to a great deal of modern writing; if history has sometimes seemed to become readily, and facilely, disposable, it has also ceased to offer consolations and companions. The essential literalism of so much recent poetry, the neo-primitive style of working everything out for the first time, stems from the conviction that the twentieth century has condemned us to a state of perpetual empiricism; even our own experience has a built-in obsolescence, sensation becomes suspect as soon as it is felt. So poetry has, with increasing frequency, found itself writing annotations and footnotes to the immediate moment; sending interim minority reports from the confused battle fields of the world outside.

Such verse grovels before the arbitrariness of the reality it conceives; it aspires, ultimately, to silence, the finishing-point of all monologues. Yet the situation offers much grander alternatives, and Peter Porter's lines at the head of this chapter give an important clue to at least one of them. 'The Last of England' is a poem which thrives on paradoxes, particularly on the basic antithesis between the 'mental' world of the head and its correspondences in the external world of fact and history. 'England' in the poem is both a place which can be left and a continuing tradition, a style of thought and feeling, which is inescapable because it is internal. And this intrinsic style seems to be represented not by a native Englishman but by Karl Marx, entombed at Highgate; like Porter himself, an immigrant. It is at once a receding quay, a planet (the most distant of imaginative entities), and something which revolves planetlike in the mind. This play of contradictions between things which are 'inside' and things which are 'outside' works like a riddle:

> What can you go away from but never leave?
> What is always foreign but necessarily native?
> What is always far away and always inside the head?

The quick answer would be 'a literary tradition'. But we can in fact only reach it by acknowledging a poetic imagination which is capable of creating the world which it observes; the fundamental, irreducible paradox of Western literary culture. 'England' in Porter's poem is not a 'real' place converted into a mythical notion, nor a 'myth' that displaces, and serves for 'reality'; It is both. And, quite unlike all the 'post-modernist' verse I have been exploring so far. Porter's poem both salutes its tradition and works assuredly within it.

We need at this point to go back briefly to Wallace Stevens; for Stevens, more than any other modern writer except Joyce, laid out a strategy for the poetic imagination in a world of arbitrary values and multiplying realities. Where Eliot and Pound set the poem at embattled loggerheads with society, and Yeats constructed a mystical cosmology for himself in which contemporary society faded to a pinpoint among his turning gyres, Stevens made the triumphant assertion that the poet as fiction-maker could exercise a godlike role in a society which had lost God and its accompanying theological certainties about the fixed position of reality. For Stevens the twentieth century was an imaginative liberation, an opened door between the perception of the poet and the shimmering, multiform essence of nature. 'The final belief,' he remarked in *Adagia*:

> is to believe in a fiction, which you know to be a fiction, there being nothing else. The exquisite truth is to know that it is a fiction and that you believe in it willingly.

Yet, at the same time, Stevens makes the seemingly paradoxical statement that this ultimate belief in fiction is grounded in a 'nature' which transcends and pre-exists the fiction-maker's inventions about it:

> Poetry has to be something more than a conception
> of the mind. It has to be a revelation of nature
> Conceptions are artificial. Perceptions are essential.

It is a fruitful contradiction of a kind that demands some sort of Platonic overworld in which it might be reconciled; and Stevens certainly has the temperament of an unconfessed Platonist. But the nearest he offers us to an overworld is the poem itself; an invention which is a perception, a fiction which has the status of natural truth. In *Notes Towards a Supreme Fiction* Stevens elaborated on the chemistry and physics of this *perceived* nature, in a verse of brilliant, sustained epigram:

> There was a muddy centre before we breathed.
> There was a myth before the myth began,
> Venerable and articulate and complete.
>
> From this the poem springs: that we live in a place
> That is not our own and, much more, not ourselves
> And hard it is in spite of blazoned days.
>
> We are the mimics. Clouds are pedagogues
> The air is not a mirror but bare board,
> Coulisse bright-dark, tragic chiaroscuro
>
> And comic colour of the rose, in which
> Abysmal instruments make sounds like pips
> Of the sweeping meanings that we add to them.

Only in artifice can we apprehend nature; the luscious imagery, drawn from painting, music, and the theatre, is both a fiction of man's invention and the mode of discovery through which he approaches that mysteriously impersonal place which neither belongs to him nor is a simple reflection of himself. Yet the way Stevens describes it, 'venerable and articulate and complete', places it clearly in the domain of art —it is *the* Supreme Fiction.

Steven's proud celebration of the enhanced power of the poet, and, indeed, of the absolute centrality of the poetic imagination, has been, if listened to at all, ignored by the majority of contemporary poets. If one wants to trace the continuing history of the supreme fiction one has to go to the novel; where Beckett, Flann O'Brien, Borges, Nabokov, and Barth have worked in prose over the vertiginous, paradoxical terrain that Stevens originally mapped out as the proper realm of poetry. It is an odd, dispiriting, but largely unarguable fact that in the last twenty years or so the novel and the poem have tended to swap places. If one is looking for low, mimetic realism—for forms which echo and assent to social circumstances and which are suicidally hospitable to fragmentation and disruption—one can endlessly find examples in contemporary verse. But if one is searching for literature which celebrates and creates imaginative life one will spend most of one's time reading novels.

For the novel has come more and more to stand as the supreme form of fiction in our time; the problem of existence, of perception and imagination, has increasingly come to seem a problem of *narration*. Even Stevens himself, for whom the meditation was the most natural and appropriate form, moved, especially in his later work, to the brink of the poem-novel; the compressed, intermittent narratives of poems like 'Sunday Morning', 'To an Old Philosopher in Rome', 'Mrs Alfred Uruguay', and others remind me of ghostly, unwritten Jamesian novels. And in 'Credences of Summer' Stevens portrays the ultimate imaginer as a novelist:

> The personae of summer play the characters
> Of an inhuman author, who meditates
> With the gold bugs, in blue meadows, late at night.
> He does not hear his characters talk. He sees
> Them mottled, in the moodiest costumes.
>
> Of blue and yellow, sky and sun, belted
> And knotted, sashed and seamed, half pales of red,
> Half pales of green, appropriate habit for
> The huge decorum, the manner of the time
> Part of the mottled mood of summer's whole.

In which the characters speak because they want
To speak, the fat, the roseate characters,
Free, for a moment, from malice and sudden cry,
Complete in a completed scene, speaking
Their parts as in a youthful happiness.

That momentary, harmonious freedom enjoyed by both
author and characters, and the appearance of leisurely, almost
wandering, accumulation of side-detail which the verse gives
as it knits together its beautifully organized symbolic whole,
is, in an important sense, *novelistic*. Its rhythm seems to be
drawn from a pattern of events, an interrelationship of people
and things, that belongs to the texture of prose fiction as it
constructs a complete society to set beside our own.

And this is just what a number of recent poets have seized
on, this sense of the inherent fictionality of life, and its possible
rendition in verse which owes a great deal to the novel. To
bargain between real and imagined worlds, to become a
maker of truthful fictions, to assert the primary function of
the imagination as it perceives the world, has meant taking on
some, at least, of the clothes of the novelist. In a number of
poems he has been writing lately Alan Brownjohn has
explored what happens when the poet consciously borrows
techniques from the novelist; inventing fictional names for
his characters, plunging into the middle of a complicated,
unrevealed narrative, adopting the tone of the narrator who
is the moral arbiter and inventor of his society. Here is the
central stanza from 'Balls of Sweetness':

When Hester Lang told Cavan Benther that
Hidden in some long spell away from him was
A week when Philip Quernier was prepared
And it happened three times (but each time one of them
Pretended) an hour was enough for Cavan's
Fury. Nor were these people heartless. It was
Not of consequence. Such oddness at such distance
Could be healed.
                    It was the world.

The verse seems to extrude its detail like a crammed nine-teenth-century novel; a saga foreshortened into a rapid, oblique telegraphic style. But in a curious way the details and made-up names become sufficient, self-contained: they close the poem around itself. The apparent social depth of the poem is deceptive; it makes for a world which has been so completely fictionalized that it takes off into a dreamlike reality of its own. Yes, one agrees, as one reads the verse, this is England, an ascertainable here-and-now; but at the same time it is a wholly imagined country, a fictive landscape which exists above and beyond the circumstances of place and time. The poem has broached—very successfully, I think—the supreme imaginative paradox.

Peter Porter, in a characteristically gamey way, opens this argument out with witty lucidity in a poem called 'Short Story', where he poses as a narrator unravelling the fate of an unsavoury young couple called Nick and Maureen:

> She could become an assistant
>   with Abacus:
> no, I'll set her up cataloguing
> maiolica in a private collection.
>
>   I'm going to give Nick
> a mild dose, but I can't stop him
>   becoming Brand Manager.
>
>   I'm wearing God's shirt.
>
>   We'll leave Maureen under the departure board
> at Waterloo looking up a train to Godalming.
>
>   The trouble is you can't write about dreams.
>
> What was caught in Surrey in the headlights?

In a realist novel it is just these sorts of detail which are used to establish the inevitability, the truth to facts, of the society of the book. In Porter's poem they announce the arbitrariness of the fiction-maker as he meddles with the nuts and bolts of his

private universe. 'Short Story' is at one level a poet's brilliant
parodic revenge on low mimesis of a hugely recognizable
kind; at the same time it is a serious trial fitting of God's shirt,
an exploration of the degrees of freedom and compulsion
experienced by the man who imagines the world he lives in.
In 'Short Story' Porter is drawing a kind of illustrative diagram,
a cartoon; in 'Europe: *An Ode*' he builds up a patchwork quilt
of European history, from the sack of Carthage to the present.
It is a marvellously rich transmutation of an entire cultural
history into a sort of comic-strip novel, a fiction of fierce jumps
in time, of chance resemblances, of the tumbling rag-bag of
the imagination:

> . . . Hefty the face of the Carthaginian, puce
>   The blood-flower in his morning steps;
>   Just a rock, towelled by tourists, yet sat
>   Down there the bum of God and a gold cat.

> . . . Sun-high, valley-served, in his dressing gown
>   Tussling with tyranny in dead March,
>   Remarkable for leaves, the great Glans foresees
>   A million Fiats in the palms, water-skis

>   Ploughing by Procida, directors' gutterals
>   On tape: 'selfishness of the poor'
>   Blows the market, money complains
>   Under Swiss peaks, the S.S. Keynes

>   Founders in a mere fathom. Worm meat
>   They all were but gave out with Gothic,
>   Clawed from Cluny, struck the sun
>   With big verbs—die for a pun

>   Was one rule, outlive any pain
>   Another. Pretty Polis, lisped the Boy King,
>   Back to back, whitebait, layer-cake;
>   Promises make Jack's jaw ache . . .

This scissors-paste-and-headlines treatment of time and geography smacks, at least faintly, of Olson's *Maximus*; but
Porter is out, at every line's turn, to underline the chanciness

of his collisions. Savage compressions push the language to
the edge of being pidgin as it gets overloaded with detail—
the detritus of history as it is carried in one's head. The verse-
form, torn between the impulse to catalogue and the ringing,
conclusive couplet that ends each stanza, has an almost
facetious tidiness about it; the air of a man desperately making
neat lists of the cluttered junk in the attic of his culture. And
in the bravura final stanza of the poem Porter achieves a point
of contemplative balance, from where he is able to hold and
contain this stew of events and characters as a single, articulated 'dream':

> Launched in the wake of our stormy mother
>   To end up on a tideless shore
>   Which this is the dream of, a place
>   Of skulls, looking history in the face.

Yet even this novelistic device, as the narrator confronts the
fabric of his own story, is seen to be an arbitrary move into
placid omniscience, a diabolical authorial liberty. What is
'this'? Is it the stanza itself, a dream of an ideal vantage-point
which would resolve the tangled lines of history in the poem?
Or is it the whole poem; are the confusions there a dream as
well? That ambiguity turns the poem into a tantalizing
imaginative labyrinth; both tale and teller are illusions which,
like a puzzle picture, we can see as real only if we choose to
follow the contours of the one and ignore the other.

   This is the real legacy of Wallace Stevens; the process of
fiction-making becomes the core of the fiction itself; feeling
and telling, as imaginative acts, turn into the stuff of actuality.
A universe of plural and competing realities is *realized* in the
plausible operations of the imagination. Yet, in a culture
hooked on empiricism, we have tended to become immune to
such self-conscious fictions, to mistake the large, imaginative
gesture for the minimal fidelities of low realism. Who, for
instance, aside from a handful of fellow-poets like Lowell and
Berryman, has really listened to what is going on in the verse

of W. D. Snodgrass, whose poems of marriage and divorce in
Heart's Needle have usually been praised simply as evidence
of honest self-revelation? He has been gratefully received as
a 'voice', credited with the sort of telephonic intimacy I was
looking at in the last chapter. Yet a poem like 'Reconstructions'
suggests something very different, and much darker. It is an
address to an absent child by a former marriage, a collage of
memories phrased in Snodgrass's artfully casual, domestic,
anecdotal style:

> . . . You offered me, one day, your doll
> To sing songs to, bubble and nurse,
> And said that was her birthday;
> You reappeared then, grabbed her away,
> Said just don't mess with her at all;
> It was your child, yours . . .

Touching enough, faithful to detail, direct . . . but the sting
lies in the fourth stanza, and the whole poem clouds and
complicates with its force:

> We are like patients who rehearse
> Old unbearable scenes
> Day after day after day.
> I memorize you, bit by bit,
> And must restore you in my verses
> To sell to magazines.

The apparent simple clarity of the verse suddenly switchbacks
into a *regressus infinitus*, a Dutch picture; the child, possess-
ively hoarding her private world, becomes hoarded in her
turn by the narrator, transformed into an image which can be
memorized 'bit by bit'; the poem itself is both a recreation of
the fiction-making that goes on in the relationship between
father and daughter, and a further fiction, inviting possession
in its own right. Yet, having recognized this, it would be a
mistake to see the poem simply as an intricate puzzle, a game
with the mechanics of perception. For it is a deeply serious
exploration of the way in which even the most intimate and

fundamental reality eludes us; the plainness of its language
is the plainness of anguish as it distils experience down in its
search for the accessible.

Snodgrass's 'private' poems do, in fact, resolve themselves
into something like a large, composite novel; experiments
in ways of telling that keep the process of narration in the
foreground as they work painstakingly over the boundaries
between memory, imagination, and present sensation. Reality
has a habit of slipping, almost accidentally, into the 'mental'
world of tone and style; and distinction between the inner
and the outer universe is always perplexing and contradictory.
The first two stanzas of a poem called 'Autumn Scene', for
instance:

> In the public gardens they are walking.
>   The skies appear correct and glum.
> Their heels click drily; they are talking.
> Behind their backs, the elms repeat some shocking
>   News of what's to come.
>
>   Otherwise, the lawns like quiet.
>   The beds are vacant, spaded, formal,
>   Where sparrows peck out a lean diet.
>   After July's sun-scattering splash and riot,
>   It's back to gray and normal.

This strikes me as much more than a straightforward pathetic
fallacy, of working out a landscape as a projection of a state of
mind. The style of bare statement, of short sentences and low-
key adjectives, pretends to an exaggerated deference to facts.
Interrupted as it is by that self-conscious anthropomorphic
whimsy about the whispering elms, it's thrown into question.
Why? Partly, I think, because Snodgrass needs a sort of
deliberate clumsiness to show through the language of the
poem, so that we can watch the fitting of words to things as
an awkward, haphazard business in which linguistic tones
and tricks are always likely to spill over into the 'objective'
world which they both create and describe. The transferred

epithet—'The skies appear correct and glum' when it is the voice of the poem itself that really appears so—becomes a symbol of the constant problem of the narrator as he tries to mediate between 'out there' and 'in here'. In a poem called 'Regraduating the Lute' Snodgrass gets as near as he has ever come to stating an aesthetic: he rehearses, in great detail, the process of bringing the instrument to a pitch of resonant maturity:

> . . . Keeping the strings
> Tuned and under tension, we gradually
>   Pare away, while playing constantly,
> All excess from behind the tempered face.
>   The way a long grief hollows the cheeks away . . .

One notices at this stage in the poem that the language is slightly out of consonance with what it says; there is a heavy, ruminative deliberation in its tone (like the clogging of the rhythm which that parenthetical phrase 'while playing con- stantly' introduces into the verse), which is at odds with the fining down of the lute itself. But it moves, towards the end, into a musical simplicity of statement, as it enforces the distinction between the well-tempered sound of the lute or the poem and its secret source in the private territory of the performer or the poet:

> . . . Its voice now
> Is equal to any in the world. We take it
>   Home to sing to or lay it on the bed.
> In any place, at any time I play,
>   Behind this face where nobody can see
> I have burned your name. To stay.

Yet, of course, in the last line the secret is opened. Or, rather, its revelation hints at a further secret, behind the polished face of the poem. The word 'this' is as ambiguous here as it was in the last stanza of Porter's poem—and for much the same reason. We are left gazing into the infinite recesses of a labyrinth.

All of these poems hinge on the profoundly dubious identity of their narrators, on a tensile play between the impersonality of the poem as fiction—a 'place not our own'—and the attempts made by their author/readers to locate a personal identity, personal feeling, on their slippery imaginative surfaces. They create legible universes—landscapes and societies which have been so completely encoded in the language of the poem that even their authors discover themselves to be strangers. The fiction and the fiction-maker peel apart from one another, as in Borges's superb sketch 'Borges and I':

> I know of Borges from the mail and see his name
> on a list of professors or in a biographical
> dictionary. I like hourglasses, maps, eighteenth
> century typography, the taste of coffee and the
> prose of Stevenson; he shares these preferences,
> but in a vain way that turns them into the attributes
> of an actor. It would be an exaggeration to say
> that ours is a hostile relationship; I live, let
> myself go on living, so that Borges may contrive
> his literature, and this literature justifies
> me.

Again the ambiguous 'this', which Borges somersaults neatly out of, in the last sentence of the piece: 'I do not know which of us has written this page'. The metaphor of the narrator as actor is one which also haunts the verse of Wallace Stevens; supreme fictions command dramaturgical analogies.

Who perceives? Who tells? From whom does imaginative authority derive?—are the continual questions of the poem-as-novel and the poem-as-theatre. They are perhaps inevitable questions, to which any work of literature that makes a total claim on our attention must address itself. Which is why I think it's worth exploring them in a poem more celebrated for its 'realism' than for its imaginative self-consciousness— Larkin's 'The Whitsun Weddings'. Larkin, even more than Snodgrass, seems to me to have suffered from his admirers;

who have shouted so loudly about the brilliant exactitude of his social detail that it is often hard to see that Larkin ever does anything else. 'The Whitsun Weddings' is surely one of the best poems to have been published since the War; it has an imaginative fullness, a sense of many dimensions, which lifts it above most of Larkin's other work, largely because, I think, it incorporates a questing realization of its own fictionality.

It is, first of all, a narrative told by a first person who lays claim both to a highly individualized identity and to a total imaginative over-view. The opening stanza makes a movement which is to become characteristic of the whole poem:

> That Whitsun, I was late getting away:
>   Not till about
> One-twenty on the sunlit Saturday
> Did my three-quarters-empty train pull out,
> All windows down, all cushions hot, all sense
> Of being in a hurry gone. We ran
> Behind the backs of houses, crossed a street
> Of blinding windscreens, smelt the fish-dock; thence
> The river's level drifting breadth began,
> Where sky and Lincolnshire and water meet.

It starts with 'I', and moves, quite abruptly, into 'We'; from possessive particularity into a communally shared experience. And at that point a slight but nagging tension enters the language of the poem. Did 'I' or 'We' *smell* the fish-dock? For the sentence begins with the general activities of the train as a vehicle and a community; when it credits the whole train with a particular sensation we're forced into making some sort of ambiguous distinction between the narrator and his fellow-passengers. Certainly when the stanza moves finally to that beautiful, decorous description of the Humber estuary we're confronted with a style that transcends both the communal events of the train and the personal details of 'I'. It has progressed, steadily and eloquently, towards a bold impersonality.

The problems of the narrator pile up during the poem, as the weddings multiply. 'Sun destroys/The interest of what's happening in the shade', and the second stanza is given over to the illuminated externals of a passing landscape. When the weddings are first perceived they are perceived inaccurately, taken for 'porters larking with the mails', while the narrator goes on reading. Then he sees the bridesmaids and families:

> Once we started, though,
> We passed them, grinning and pomaded, girls
> In parodies of fashion, heels and veils,
> All posed irresolutely, watching us go,
>
> As if out on the end of an event
>   Waving good-bye
> To something that survived it . . .

But it is the narrator who has got the event back to front, seeing it tail-end first; for him it is the people on the platform, not the newlyweds, who have 'survived'. And the poem subsequently opens out into a proliferating series of separate versions of the event: the narrator's, with his Larkinesque sensitivity to the vulgar detail—

> The fathers with broad belts under their suits
> And seamy foreheads; mothers loud and fat;
> An uncle shouting smut; and then the perms
> The nylon gloves and jewellery-substitutes . . .

—then the fathers', who 'had never known/ Success so huge and wholly farcical'; the women's, who 'shared/The secret like a happy funeral'; and the girls', who 'stared/At a religious wounding'. One ought to notice that the narrator's original version is incompatible with his later ability to get inside the heads of the very people whom he was, moments before, seeing merely as components of a comic-squalid mass. The tension has elaborated to a rich and subtle conflict between 'I', 'We', and 'They'.

> Free at last,
> And loaded with the sum of all *they* saw,
> *We* hurried towards London . . .
>
> [*my italics*]

Yet the 'sum of all they saw' belongs only to the poem; not to the participants in the weddings, nor even to the personalized narrator. It is solely in his role as 'poet' that he can make any claim to possessing the totality of the experience. 'We' has turned into the community, not just of the train, but of the poem, its author, and its readers.

The last stanza and a half build up to a pitch of extraordinary imaginative resonance as they bring together all the separate versions of the poem into a single chord:

>   None
> Thought of the others they would never meet
> Or how their lives would all contain this hour.
> I thought of London spread out in the sun,
> Its postal districts packed like squares of wheat:
>
> There we were aimed. And as we raced across
>   Bright knots of rail
> Past standing Pullmans, walls of blackened moss
> Came close, and it was nearly done, this frail
> Travelling coincidence; and what it held
> Stood ready to be loosed with all the power
> That being changed can give. We slowed again,
> And as the tightened brakes took hold, there swelled
> A sense of falling, like an arrow-shower
> Sent out of sight, somewhere becoming rain.

Again, narrator and couples are separated, and the containing hour becomes something perceived impersonally; belonging to the train and to the poem. In the final stanza immediate details, which locate the event as a collision of particular circumstances, are absorbed into an embracing general statement; 'this frail/Travelling coincidence'—another *this*—is the poem itself, an articulate fiction which transports, and delivers to a destination, the body of private perceptions of which it is composed. They too are changed and loosed; married to one another, liberated from being merely separate details, partial perceptual slices of a splintered world. The poem, like a marriage or a train journey, transforms, contains, brings into being a new, communal life. In the last four lines the nature of that life is hinted at; it is as mysterious, as prone to disappearance, as indifferent to the grimy detail or the private person, as weather.

Entertaining as it might be as a gambit in a literary party-game, I am not trying to make Larkin out to be an unrecon-structed neo-Platonist nor the architect of a Borgesian maze. Yet where the muttering, breathing, and shouting exponents of the new mimesis, from Black Mountain to Newcastle upon Tyne, have shied away from the poem as fiction, let alone supreme fiction, on the grounds that such concerns are an unmanly, 'academic', escape from all-important realism, Larkin's poem demonstrates, I think, that the dimension of fiction is inescapable. The act of perception, of imagination, cannot help but bring the writer to the vertiginous brink of that place where 'seeing' and 'making' shimmer into an infinite depth of liberating confusion. And even 'realism' leads there, or should, were it not for the fact that so many of its contemporary practitioners are firmly and solipsistically bent on staying at home. The poet, whatever his professed humility before facts, or democratic convictions, is a man fated to wear God's shirt, whether he likes it or not.

9

Collecting the Poem

My lines swell up and spank like the bow of a yacht;
outside, the break-through of the Broadway bookstores,
outside, the higher voltage of studenten,
the Revolution seeking her professor . . .
It's life in death to be typed, bound, delivered,
lie on reserve like the old Boston *British Poets*,
hanged for keeping meter . . .

ROBERT LOWELL, *Notebook*

So far I've been examining only particular poems and fragments of poems, and the individual poets themselves have
tended to get hurried along the line of the general argument.
It seems useful at this stage to introduce the larger frame of the
collection and to bring together some of the major themes I've
been identifying by looking at three of the most important
books of verse published during 1969 and 1970: Ted Hughes's
Crow, Charles Tomlinson's *The Way of a World*, and Robert
Lowell's *Notebook*. My choice of 'important' collections may,
I am aware, look suspiciously like a thankful return to home
cooking after a roundabout tour of such exotic confections
as concrete/disposable/wrap-around/instant verse. Yet these
three writers are all deeply and self-consciously immersed in
the play of contemporary language and society; their poetry,
although it speaks from somewhere near the literary, if not the
cultural, centre of things, incorporates, argues with, at least
takes notice of, many of the radical styles I have described.

Indeed, when *Notebook* was published in England a re-
viewer in *The Times Literary Supplement* attacked it for what
he diagnosed as a modish sloppiness; Lowell had broken his
pact with his own strict talent and made a vulgar concession
to the temporary, the raw. P. N. Furbank glossed the point

more sympathetically in *The Listener* when he wrote that Lowell had, 'with calculated recklessness, staked everything on the provisional'. Nearly 400 jagged, unrhymed 'sonnets' compose what Lowell calls 'the story of my life'; *Notebook* is a single poem, a discontinuous, broken-textured fiction. It looks back to the Elizabethan sonnet-sequence, and looks sideways to the twentieth-century novel:

> The time is a summer, an autumn, a winter, a spring,
> another summer. I began working sometime in June 1967
> and finished in June 1970. My plot rolls with the
> seasons, but one year is confused with another. I have
> flashbacks to what I remember, and fables inspired by
> impulse. Accidents threw up subjects, and the plot
> swallowed them—famished for human chances.

And the 'plot' of *Notebook*—its imaginative shape and direction, its brilliant conceits and inventions—counterpoints all the accidents of public and personal history through which it charts out its course. Lowell has chosen the most difficult and compromised of all poetic stances; he wears God's shirt and simultaneously submits himself to the erratic and irrational currents of the world. The problem of telling, of making through narration, is constantly harnessed to the demands of an external universe which seems intermittently legible; the super-novel or super-movie in which we are all characters, and whose script varies from supreme symbolic lucidity to the indecipherable.

> This year runs out in the movies, it must be written
> in bad, straightforward, unscanning sentences—
> mine were downtrodden, branded on the backs of carbons,
> lines, words, letters nailed to letters, words, lines;
> the typescript looked like a Rosetta Stone.
> A year's black pages. Its hero *hero demens*
> forcing his ship past soundings to the passage—
> ill-starred of men and crossed by his fixed stars.
> The slush-ice on the east water of the Hudson
> is rose-heather this New Year sunset; the open channel,
> bright sky, bright sky, carbon scarred with ciphers.

Yet out of the confusions and repetitions the sonnet itself is able, in its hinging seventh line, to retrieve a symmetrical pattern: 'lines, words, letters nailed to letters, words, lines'— a pattern made up of linguistic and literary terms, like shuffled counters. The relationship between the scarred carbon and the bright sky is one of perpetual paradox; the poem creates, and mimics, and contradicts the world. Beside the world's hangover clarity the poem is so many black marks; yet it is in the order and rhythm and metaphoric invention of the sentence that the world achieves its existence. More particularly, the poet himself becomes the created hero, afloat in his own written forms; the author and the victim of his own fiction. In 'Reading Myself' Lowell teases this out in a metaphor which brings him to a point of ultimacy where the sentence disintegrates, leaving the two halves of the paradox to confront one another across a row of dots:

> No honeycomb is built without a bee
> adding circle to circle, cell to cell,
> the wax and honey of a mausoleum—
> this round dome proves its maker is alive,
> the corpse of such insect lives preserved in honey,
> prays that the perishable work live long
> enough for the sweet-tooth bear to desecrate—
> this open book . . . my open coffin.

The sugary mausoleum is also 'this round dome', the conventional poetic synonym for both the theatre and the world, or the world-as-theatre; the labouring insect is also God. And who is the 'sweet-tooth bear'? If it is the reader, then it is also the author, reading himself, an eerie party to his own nightmare life-in-death.

The 'life story' in *Notebook* is never merely the story *of* a life; it is life *as* story, as fiction, in the full, heightened inflexion given to that word by Stevens.

> Reading this book to four or five that night
> at Cuernavaca, till the lines glowered and glowed,
> and my friend, Monsignor Illich, ascetic donkey,

braying, 'Will you die, when the book is done?'
It stopped my heart, and not my mouth. I said,
'I have begun to wonder.'

Lowell's life and his book are profoundly identified with one
another; it is as if a Faustian bargain had been struck between
the author and his work. *Notebook*, like Melville's *Moby Dick*,
is a monument to the dream that a man might create himself
by the exercise of his will, his imagination, in collusion with
the forces of external reality. Its rough tempo, its savage
breaks of syntax, its lapses into prosy doggerel, its sudden,
unaccountable leaps into metaphor, are part of the essential
harmony of that dream; of a life achieving the order of fiction,
of fiction achieving the disorder of life.

More completely than any other poem or novel I have read,
Notebook realizes the multiform texture of twentieth-century
society, and realizes it without cowering before it. Lowell has
made the ultimate artistic sacrifice, and used his life, not as the
subject of indulgent autobiography, but as a sensitive, finally
impersonal, membrane, on which the world reverberates and
becomes articulate. The private character who lives through
the verse—the father, husband, lover, cigarette-smoker,
hypochondriac, rememberer, meditator, imaginer—is, like
us all, an insecure inhabitant of the world of public events.
Vietnam, the Middle East, race riots, political assassinations,
party conventions, demonstrations, jostle in his consciousness against the fragmentary, perceived detail, the domestic
incident, the nagging fear of the death-rattle in his lungs. The
processes of logic, of rationality, come abruptly up against the
iridescent flashes of imagination. The intuitive arrangement
of the separate sonnets in the collection, with their jumps and
sidetracks, as they follow the quirky, random line of the
private sensibility, is set against the pursuing tone of argument within the individual poem as it tracks down a metaphor
or chases an idea. Sometimes this confrontation happens
within a single sonnet, sometimes it happens in the spaces be-

tween a group of poems. There is always a profound sense of
the bifurcation of consciousness; the intricately worked
conceit suddenly loses itself in doggerel; doggerel suddenly
rises to perfect conceit.

Lowell has always been interested in the transcription as a
poetic form; rearrangements of other people's language in
verse. In *Notebook* he borrows chunks from letters, conversations, other literature, and these give the poem a continuous
diet of roughage; a strong, sometimes violent, sense of the
imaginative resistance offered by external reality. An un-
identified woman friend writes on 'Publication Day':

> 'Dear Robert: I wish you were not a complete stranger,
> I wish I knew something more about your mercy,
> could total your minimum capacity
> for empathy—this varies so much from genius.
> Can you fellow-suffer for a turned-down book?'

The sonnet form and the line-breaks belong to Lowell, while
the words belong to the woman. The poem in its entirety both
absorbs this external language and grates against it; the
emotional tone of the transcription, as well as its vocabulary,
eats ironically away at its context. Lowell's ability to incorporate the letter into *Notebook* is the very reverse of
'empathy' for it accentuates the way in which the poem is able
to make, and recognize, boundaries between its own imaginative life and the world outside.

Such incorporations stake out the perimeter of the universe
of the poem; that area where consciousness and imagination
can do almost nothing with experience except to acknowledge
its existence. 'A nihilist,' remarks Lowell, in a sonnet called
'The Nihilist as Hero', 'has to live in the world as is.' Perception and invention are sporadic; they sputter into life, and as
quickly fade, and *Notebook* thrives on their waywardness. If,
on occasion, experience can be only broken up into lines,
there are other times when it seems richly pliable, amenable
to metaphor and the luminous association caught in a magical

collision of words. Here are extracts from two poems, both of which work in freakishly swift transitions, pulling a splay of experiences into the magnetic field of the verse:

> Lying in bed, letting the bright, white morning
> rise to mid-heaven through a gag of snow,
> through highschool, through college, through fall-term
>   vacation—
> I've slept so late here, snow has stubbled my throat;
> students in their hundreds rise from the beehive,
> swarm-mates; they have clocks and instincts, make
> classes. In the high sky, a parochial school,
> the top floors looking like the Place des Vosges—
> a silk stocking, blown thin as smog, coils in a twig-fork,
> dangling a wire coathanger, rapier-bright—
> a long throw for a hard cold day . . . wind lifting
> the stocking like the lecherous, lost leg.
>
> Even in August, it turned autumn . . . all
> Prospect Pond could harbour. No sound; no talk;
> the dead match nicked the water and expired,
> a target-circle on inverted sky,
> nature's mirror . . . just a little cold!
> Our day was cold and short, love, and its sun,
> numb as the red carp, twenty inches long,
> panting, a weak old dog, below a smashed
> oar floating from a metal dock. . . .

The dash, the comma, the semicolon, and the row of dots are Lowell's characteristic punctuation-points. They are all means of juxtaposing, splicing together, fragments of life which only assume meaning when they are knitted into pattern and metaphor. So the bedroom junk in the first quotation grows suddenly animate and articulate, and in the second, sun and carp, the couple and the mirror-surface of the pond, are discovered, with all the force of temporariness, to be enacting a grave symbolic game. Reading these poems, one can't miss the clutter of words; the way in which each line seems to be straining at both ends to contain its contents. It's as if the verse had to provide all the confusion of raw materials, the chance bits and pieces, out of which image and metaphor are made. The throat stubbled with snow, and the carp seen as 'a weak old dog' are figurations which seem to just happen; the accidental linkages of a mind retrieving and working over its experience. In this sense the sonnets in *Notebook* are all 'dramatic'; they re-enact the processes of thinking and re-membering. Making the poem itself becomes the exercise of consciousness in its most difficult and liberated form; nothing less, in fact, than life.

This helps to explain why, in poetic as well as in personal terms, *Notebook* is so haunted by death. Dying and its attend-ants—the doctor's cardiograph, the furniture of hospitals, the obscure symptom of an undiagnosed or unconfirmed disease—constantly enter the poems to threaten their exis-tence. When the poem breaks down under the force of its own perceptions, or ends in silence, a death has occurred. And the mortality of Lowell's chosen form—its constant breakdowns, lapses into inactivity, and dissolution into the surrounding white space of the book—works as a continual dark reminder that making the poem, like living in the twentieth century, is fragilely sustained by grace against all odds.

> At this point of civilization, this point of the world,
> the only satisfactory companion we
> can imagine is death— this morning, skin lumping in my throat,
> I lie here, heavily breathing, the soul of New York.

Lowell seems to me to have justified, miraculously, the con-ceit of that last line; in *Notebook* he has written an extra-ordinary epic, outfacing the literal and figurative deaths that surround the poem. Like *The Waste Land*, *Notebook*, despite its anguished embrace of the provisional, achieves a kind of epic finality. After publishing the first edition of the book Lowell continued to add sonnets to it; there are over ninety extra poems in the English edition of 1970, and succeeding editions may well contain many more. But the poem itself, as an embodiment of the notion of life-as-book, seriously aspires to the point beyond which no more poetry can be written. I don't believe that any verse of the last twenty or thirty years comes closer than *Notebook* to being a masterpiece.

In the shadows beneath *Notebook* there is the rumble of the millennium, the threat of a formless ultimacy, a bleak, decisive ending. And, as Charles Tomlinson remarks in a poem called 'Against Extremity', 'The time is in love with endings.' Tomlinson's own poems are firmly in love with middles, with the landscapes and solidities through which the human consciousness manoeuvres. In 'The Chances of Rhyme', an elegant, sharp essay in verse aesthetics which both pre-dates and chimes with Davie's *Epistles*, Tomlinson slaps irritatedly at the ideology of poetic brinkmanship:

> Why should we speak
> Of art, of life, as if the one were all form
>   And the other all Sturm-und-Drang? And I think
> Too, we should confine to Crewe or to Mow
>   Cop, all those who confuse the fortuitousness
> Of art with something to be met with only
>   At extremity's brink, reducing thus
> Rhyme to a kind of rope's end, a glimpsed grass
>   To be snatched at as we plunge past it—

It's a slap which whistles close by Lowell's ear; and *The Way of a World* turns into a kind of recurrent soliloquy by a poet working out a style of survival, surrounded by millennialists, prophets of doom, and necrophiliacs of silence. At the heart of Tomlinson's poems there is indeed a vein of commonsensical, liberal, philosophizing Englishness; a conviction that both nature and society are essentially intractable, and that the business of the poet is to attend to the details and dynamics of the real. But where such preoccupations tended, amongst the Movement poets for instance, to be part of a web of the sort of unstated assumptions that might be tacitly agreed between gentlemen, in Tomlinson's work they're argued on the surface; and argued in the international context of modern painting, poetry, and music. His refusal to consent to post-modernism as a style of radicalism and extremity is not born of the insular prejudice which Larkin rolled into his tongue-in-cheek exclamation, '*Foreign* poetry? No!' One of the central poems in this collection is 'Prometheus', in which a listener in an English provincial town hears a radio broadcast of Scriabin's tone-poem; the thunderous apocalypse of the music and Scriabin's characteristically modernist belief in the power of art to transform, or provide an ending for, life and history are posed against their contemporary auditor with his radio set.

> Summer darkens, and its climbing
>   Cumulae, disowning our scale in the zenith,
> Electrify this music: the evening is falling apart.
>   Castles-in-air; on earth: green, livid fire.
> The radio simmers with static to the strains
>   Of this mock last-day of nature and of art.

The poem is full of interlocking frames. There is, at one remove, Scriabin's 'Prometheus', which is contained within Tomlinson's 'Prometheus'; while both work in 'scales' which are 'disowned' by a nature which is, of course, a constituent part of Tomlinson's own poem. And the problem of scale gets even more complicated when the radio-set itself can grow, in the poem, to a conceptual size and importance that makes it rival both the climbing cumulae and the music which comes out of it. We are in the middle of a fundamental perceptual muddle; baffled at the profusion of experience with which we have to deal. And from the second stanza onwards the poem takes off into an associative sidetrack of its own, meditating on the apocalyptic impulses of the Russian Revolution, on Trotsky, Lenin, Kerensky, and Blok. Music and history intertwine, but the purity of extremism is lost in the proliferation of events and consequences.

Prometheus came down

In more than orchestral flame and Kerensky fled
Before it. The babel of continents gnaws now
And tears at the silk of those harmonies that seemed
So dangerous once. You dreamed an end
Where the rose of the world would go out like a close in
music.

By this stage the language of the poem becomes overburdened
by its own diversity. Its insistent metaphorization and its
equally insistent impulse to argument give it a troubling and
troubled opacity. Yet I think we are asked to listen to the poem
as an alternative style to that of Scriabin's music; its painfully
'talky' rhythms are juxtaposed against the millennial simplicities of the orchestra. In the final two stanzas Tomlinson
manages to achieve a remarkable clarity of statement; the
poem, quite suddenly, provides him with a vantage-point
from which the confused noises of art, nature, history, and
society can be heard to compose a curiously Augustan
harmony:

Scriabin, Blok, men of extremes,
History treads out the music of your dreams
Through blood, and cannot close like this
In the perfection of anabasis. It stops. The trees
Continue raining though the rain has ceased
In a cooled world of incessant codas:
Hard edges of the houses press
On the after-music senses, and refuse to burn,
Where an ice-cream van circulates the estate
Playing Greensleeves, and at the city's
Stale new frontier even ugliness
Rules with the cruel mercy of solidities.

What has happened is that one style has been, more or less
arbitrarily, substituted for another. Reality conveniently
reasserts itself in a 'cooled world' of neat, rectangular council
houses; but it is a reality which is just as conventional, even

in its paradoxes (like the dandyish and mannered 'cruel mercy' of those solidities), as the apocalypticism which it is supposed to displace.

'Prometheus' is, I think, a very interesting poem, whose failures are as significant as its successes. Never before has Tomlinson's kind of realism—a fundamental honesty to objects—needed to be justified with such anguished self-consciousness. So many of the poems in *The Way of a World* bring into play a formidable equipment of aesthetic theory and argumentative energy, and then manage to squeeze from them only a few small drops of the consolations of realism. His poetry is always raising questions to which his answers come as anticlimaxes. 'Are we the lords or limits/Of this teeming horde?', he asks in 'Adam', as he puzzles out the relationship between our words and the things to which we assign them. It is a question that eats away at his verse; the destructive riddle which goads the modern writer who must both believe in a reality beyond himself and wonder whether he may not have merely created that reality by locating it in his language. At the level of theoretical argument Tomlinson's poems tend to break themselves up; they draw the reader into a vortex of unanswerables without sufficiently recognizing or dramatizing their own uncertain, paradoxical movements.

Just occasionally there is a streak of visionary certainty in his verse, in which his own preoccupations are accommodated and made concrete. In 'Descartes and the Stove' Tomlinson sets the philosopher in a world of brilliant and pressing sensation, beautifully notated in a sequence of lines whose metrical exactitude and objective detail form an exquisite tribute to the solidity of the real:

> The foot-print
> He had left on entering, had turned
> To a firm dull gloss, and the chill
> Lined it with a fur of frost. Now
> The last blaze of day was changing
> All white to yellow, filling

With bluish shade the slots and spoors
    Where, once again, badger and fox would wind
Through the phosphorescence.

Then, at the end, the poem focuses down on Descartes
himself:

                    The great mind
Sat with his back to the unreasoning wind
    And doubted, doubted at his ear
The patter of ash and, beyond, the snow-bound farms,
    Flora of flame and iron contingency
And the moist reciprocation of his palms.

The lonely poignance of the doubting philosopher, encircled
by the riches of his own sensations, broods over the collection.
Like Descartes, Tomlinson is drawn both ways, and at its best
his poetry contains and articulates that tension; it explores
the predicament of the man whom history has turned into a
relativist and who yet sees and feels and smells and hears the
world whose existence he has been taught to doubt.

Tomlinson venerates both language and things, and the
subtle grammar of the relationship between man as language-
maker and the inarticulate elements with which he negotiates.
The first poem in the book, 'Swimming Chenango Lake',
explores this idea, in that supple, dignified, strangely *public*
tone in which Tomlinson seems most at ease:

For to swim is also to take hold
    On water's meaning, to move in its embrace
And to be, between grasp and grasping, free.
    He reaches in-and-through to that space
The body is heir to, making a where
    In water, a possession to be relinquished
Willingly at each stroke. The image he has torn
    Flows-to behind him, healing itself,
Lifting and lengthening, splaying like the feathers
    Down an immense wing whose darkening spread
Shadows his solitariness: alone, he is unnamed
    By this baptism, where only Chenango bears a name

In a lost language he begins to construe—
    A speech of densities and derisions, of half-
Replies to the questions his body must frame
    Frogwise across the all but penetrable element.

The syntax of the verse follows the slow, muscular, repetitive movements of the swimmer; it too conjures the resistance of nature and pushes against it. The poem almost has the flavour of a metaphysical conceit as it elaborates its mimetic form; it is, at every point, doing what it says—even to the line-break separating 'half-/Replies'. And this is where Tomlinson joins, and may have learned from, the Black Mountaineers; there is in his poetry the constant attempt to endow language with the physical solidity of a medium like clay. In his short-lined poems he breaks his lines so that they enforce a jumpy, contingent rhythm on experience; and, interestingly, the experiences of the verse—driving a car, watching Mexican dancers, talking to a barber, seeing tramps in a station restaurant—seem to be chosen as diagrams of the way in which 'life' can proffer a 'natural metre'. Here is a section from 'Terminal Tramps':

The drunk walks
suddenly half
the room's length
balanced tensely
by the strength of one
determination—to make it;
and to complete the demonstration
he flings with a total
accuracy into the slot
of a litter bin
his emptied bottle.
Her babble stops him.
He attends, and for the first
time sees her;
she takes him in,
her din rises

raging against the mere
shape he makes there:
it is her voice not she
gets up to accost him
and to demand her civil
answer . . .

As a demonstration of how a poetic arrangement of language
can work as a score for a sequence of physical activities, this
works with the precision of a good textbook; and that seems
to me to be Tomlinson's trouble. Too often, like Olson and the
more programmatic of the concretists, his interest in linguistic
and poetic theory drives him to write poems which are little
more than illustrations; a kind of 'action criticism'. He knows
what he is doing so well that he cannot help telling you, too
much of the time. One feels that too many of the footnotes, the
technical dialogues which the writer must have with himself—
and should, most of the time, keep to himself—have climbed
up on to the surface of the poem.

   That self-consciousness and its attendant dangers are
profoundly characteristic of contemporary verse. The necessity to justify the medium of the poem, its means, and even its
bare existence, has forced a large number of individual poems
into a position where they do almost nothing except make
polemical apologies for coming into being at all. Indeed, the
functions of explanation and analysis which literature was
once happy to leave as the province of literary criticism are
increasingly being performed by literature itself. The concretists, minimalists, and Black Mountaineers are clearly so
busy producing exegeses and manifestos that it would be
polite to wait a few decades before we get the actual poems.
What is interesting is that a British poet like Tomlinson, whose
poetic practice seems fundamentally conservative, should be
impelled in the same, perilous direction.

   In an important sense the force of both Lowell's and Tomlinson's best poems stems from the way in which they keep

up a continual dialogue with the society that surrounds them. They borrow its language, deal with its public and aesthetic issues, play against its assumptions; society is always present in their verse, even if only to generate a powerful current of resistance. When Ted Hughes's *Crow* was published in 1970 many reviewers greeted it as a triumph because it seemed, at first glance at least, to have got beyond all that; to have moved into a further dimension, beyond society, beyond extremity. (My own initial response to the book, written shortly after it came out, is at the end of Chapter 2; I haven't revised it, although I think, with the hindsight of four months, that I was probably wrong.) Hughes himself helped to set the seal on his fairly rapturous critical reception in an interview published in *London Magazine* in January 1971. There he announced that both Christianity and civilization were dead, and that he stood knee-deep in their rubble with a kind of calm joy. He was against rationalism and for 'the elemental power circuit of the Universe'; poetry is 'the record of just how the forces of the Universe try to redress some balance disturbed by human error'. The function of the poet in society was to be that of a witch-doctor, or shaman; summoned in a trance to the spirit-world, yet able to survive and return, like Ishmael, as narrator-hero. The interview itself is a marvellous piece of myth-making. Like Yeats in *A Vision*, Hughes weaves a fictive universe around his poetry; the whole of human history is elaborately bent and shaped into an inevitable perch for *Crow*.

The poems in *Crow* are, in Hughes's words, 'the songs that a Crow would sing. In other words, songs with no music whatsoever, in a super-simple and a super-ugly language.' They tell, in a fragmentary sequence, the 'apocryphal' story of Crow, 'created by God's nightmare's attempt to improve on man.' They make up a black Bible; rehearsing the Creation, the Fall, the Crucifixion, and the collapse of Christian civilization by turning them all back-to-front, like a voodoo incantation.

> They were usually something of a shock to write. Mostly
> they wrote themselves quite rapidly, the story was a
> sort of machine that assembled them, and several of them
> that seem ordinary enough now arrived with a sense of
> having done something . . . tabu.

This is an extremely interesting remark, and it's worth re-
membering that a taboo, by definition, is a boundary established by social convention. I think that the *Crow* poems are
profoundly about the illicit euphoria of venturing into the
territory of the taboo, and that this makes them essentially
social, in a way that has been under-acknowledged by both
their author and most of their readers. A great deal of their
energy, their celebrated 'violence', springs from the tension
that they tap between the conventionally permitted and the
forbidden. Their language, far from being post-Christian,
post-civilized, is a language obsessed by institutional rules.
They munch nonchalantly away at the apple in the garden,
not because they have not heard of, or do not care about,
God's injunction, but because they know that it will get them
into trouble.

Hughes finds a basic argot for his poems in the rhythms,
vocabulary, and syntax of the Old Testament—or, rather,
those bits of it which have been made so familiar through
church services and school assemblies that they provide a
basic grammar of reverential, ritual effects. The strings of *who
begat's*, the Genesis style of narration, with all the intervening
causes left out, the sonorous, liturgical catalogue, the *And X
said unto Y* ceremonial dialogue, the rhetorical repetition—
these supply a context, a ground bass, against which to sound
the new, forbidden noises. Occasionally the poems make an
exact parody of particular Biblical passages, like this first
stanza of 'Conjuring in Heaven', which is a blasphemous
rewrite of the opening words of St John's Gospel:

> So finally there was nothing.
> It was put inside nothing.
> Nothing was added to it

> And to prove it didn't exist
> Squashed flat as nothing with nothing.

At the end of the poem, after more extravagant games with 'nothing' taking the place of 'logos', Hughes blows a vulgar raspberry at the rhetoric, by introducing a tone of crude, Hollywood-clipped, tough-talk:

> And so it was dropped. Prolonged applause in Heaven.

> It hit the ground and broke open—

> There lay Crow, cataleptic.

There's something schoolboyish about that 'Prolonged applause in Heaven', and, without wanting to isolate this particular poem unfairly (it is one of the weakest in the collection), it does point to an essential feature of *Crow*: the whole sequence does work as a slapstick rhetorical comedy. These are *funny* poems, in a way that any child who has enjoyèd puncturing a grand style by filling it with incongruous details would recognize. There is, in them all, an element of simple naughtiness as they thumb their noses at the theological and historical pieties from which they derive.

Jokes, of course, are fundamentally related to what is taboo. We make jokes about the dangerous and uncertain edges of our existence—sex, divinity, and excretion are constant joke-sources. And *Crow* is full of ritual jokes of this kind, of the laughter that tames by cruelty, humiliation, and contempt. In 'Crow's Song of Himself' there's a liturgical account of the Creation: God makes, in order, gold, diamond, alcohol, money, day, fruit, and man, while at the same time He tortures Crow in various unpleasant and specific ways. Then—

> When God tried to chop Crow in two
> He made woman
> When God said: 'You win, Crow,'
> He made the Redeemer.

When God went off in despair
Crow stropped his beak and started in on the two thieves.

The poem ends with what is, in its tone and structure, clearly a comedian's punch-line. Lying just behind it is that whole genre of sex jokes which celebrate the virility of a notorious horn who finishes up, after he has humiliated every available woman, with a massive, contemptuous erection. This particular mythic hero figures in summer shows on pierheads everywhere; his function is to trample merrily over all our fears of impotence and sexual bungling. In *Crow* he has got religion.

This is, I think, much more than a passing, superficial resemblance. Crow's incredible, indiscriminate appetites, his 'laughing' and 'grinning' (words that endlessly repeat themselves through the sequence), and his bedraggled cockiness—his proletarian powers of survival—give him a great deal in common with the battered, rakish clerks and travelling salesmen (each with one black eye and stockinged feet, often clutching a limp carnation) who are the Don Juans of the world of Donald McGill. Like them, he stands for 'getting by', 'having a good time in spite of it all', 'look after today and let tomorrow take care of itself', 'go in and get it while you can'. Only while the raggy clerks and salesmen operate among the mean, penny-pinching *mores* of the furtive, embarrassed sex of the English, pre-War lower middle class, Crow flaps perkily around the waste land of an exhausted Christian civilization. And just as the libidinous sex joke only unconsciously reveals the fear, the essential respect, which underlies it, so *Crow's* blasphemous laughter betrays the fact that we still have beliefs and pieties which can be outraged or, if you prefer it, liberated.

If blasphemy is one way of venturing into the taboo, the inversion of literary form is another; and Hughes uses the çomic strip and the thriller—'low' styles—to prick the gross rhetorical bubble of metaphysics and Christian myth. In 'Crow's Account of St George' there's a characteristic passage:

> Something grabs at his arm. He turns. A bird-head,
> Bald, lizard-eyes, the size of a football, on two staggering
>   bird-legs
> Gapes at him all the seams and pleats of its throat,
> Clutching at the carpet with horny feet,
> Threatens. He lifts the chair—fear lifts him—
> He smashes the egg-shell object to a blood-rag,
> A lumping sprawl, he tramples the bubbling mess.
> The shark-face is screaming at the doorway
> Opening its fangs. The chair again—

The sensitive adult poetry-reader might well recoil from this as 'violence'; again, a child wouldn't. If you imagine it as a story-line in *Classics Illustrated*, or as a purple patch in a novel by Raymond Chandler, the conventions immediately click into place around it. The hyperboles, the domestic similes, the parenthetic breathlessness of the syntax, the use of metonyms for talking about the villain ('Bird-head', 'Shark-face'), are all part of a thoroughly recognizable jokey-tough texture. A little later in the poem one hits a splendid Chandlerism in the couplet

> And as hacking a path through thicket he scatters
> The lopped segments, the opposition collapses.

That tight-lipped circumlocution is yet another stylistic feature which Crow shares with Chandler's hard-bitten ex-cop Philip Marlowe. Indeed, both are figures of survival, clear-sighted tough guys in a world of rackets and phoneys; their capacity to deal with that world is vested in their control of a language that mixes hyperbole and understatement in equal parts—hyperbole for the nightmare violence they encounter, understatement for cutting through the highly coloured tissue of lies and false reasons in which violence comes dressed.

But it is a language of consistent, if ambiguous, comedy. For Hughes—and Chandler, for that matter—knows how to exploit, for all it's worth, the anarchic paradox of the mirror-relationship between the poem or novel and the world. A terrible world, where nature is always vengeful, bloody, and unreasonable, is turned, when it enters the language of the poem, into a series of triumphant, comic simplicities. It is translated into a rhetoric of thunderous statements and impossible collisions, a grammar in which words are licensed to do almost anything. But the relation of the violence of the poem to the violence of the world outside is that of the dodgem-car circuit to the motor accidents on the road beyond the fairground. One sees this most clearly in *Crow* when Hughes's obvious relish in what he's doing comes to the forefront of the poem. The opening of 'In Laughter', for instance:

> Cars collide and erupt luggage and babies
> In laughter
> The steamer upends and goes under saluting like a stuntman
> In laughter
> The nosediving aircraft concludes with a boom
> In laughter
> People's arms and legs fly off and fly on again
> In laughter
> The haggard mask on the bed rediscovers its pang
> In laughter, in laughter
> The meteorite crashes
> With extraordinary ill-luck on the pram

Extraordinary bad luck for the baby, perhaps, but it is a stroke of fantastic good fortune for the poem; almost as much of a windfall as being able to make arms and legs not only fly off, but fly on again, as well. One is reminded of the European concretists' notion of the poem as a *Spielraum*, a playfield. For Hughes is like someone who has been allowed, for the magical duration of the poem, to use an abattoir as an adventure playground. But we never stop seeing that it is all based on a trick, a joke, an aesthetic paradox; the taboo has been broached only in dream.

In March 1971 Roy Fuller took Hughes to task in *The Listener* for *Crow's* sadistic imagery and the pathological violence of its language. Discussing the *London Magazine* interview, Fuller wrote that Hughes

> is prepared to say farewell to the civilization on
> which [a moral judgment of his work] would depend.
> If I read his remarks aright (not an easy matter)
> he has succumbed (as Nietzsche and Spengler succumbed)
> to the fallacy that the worse the age the more men
> must adapt to it.

I think Fuller takes *Crow*—as, indeed, many of the book's most ardent admirers have taken it—too literally, as if what it talked about and what it did were synonymous. It seems to me that the collection is most marred by the way in which it cushions the violence it speaks of. Hughes himself may be prepared to say farewell to civilization, but *Crow* is profoundly rooted to it. The shocks and insults and blasphemies of the poems are libidinous fantasies, the night-thoughts of a society which knows its own boundaries. Significantly, *Crow* had to be reprinted within days of publication, and has become—a very rare thing indeed, for a book of poems—a best-seller. Civilization, at any rate, seems to have found its violence remarkably easy to swallow.

10
Society and the Poem

The pluralism of contemporary verse, with its accompanying scatter of poetic ideologies, has made for an atmosphere thick in plots and delusions. Schools and movements flourish; so do conspiracy theories of literary history. It has perhaps become rather harder than ever before for anyone to feel certain about literary value. At least, bad poems are, as always, being hailed as masterpieces, while good ones, as always, are being shoved aside; but the inverted proportion seems even higher than a cynical view of the absurdities of criticism and the puff system might lead one to expect. During the course of writing this book I began to wonder quite seriously whether we had not been rendered constitutionally incapable of doing anything more than mildly preferring some poems to others—made insensible by prolonged exposure to works of minor, if irascible, genius. It's important at this stage, I think, to look at the transmission systems and communications channels of contemporary verse—that oddly wired-up bundle of loops and short-circuits through which poems find audiences and make reputations.

In the mimeo'd mags and broadsheets there's a widespread and deeply felt myth about the 'stranglehold' of the 'literary establishment'—an august and dusty body dedicated to the asphyxiation of 'live poetry' by internment in the universities and weekly reviews. Jeff Nuttall, in *Bomb Culture*, puts the case in a somewhat wistful past tense:

> The rebel styles in literature were blocked out of publishing,
> out of libraries, out of serious discussion, by the extensive
> influence of the universities who are too idle to reform
> their critical axioms and therefore try to preserve the
> critical status quo.

Michael Horovitz, baying back at the critics of his *Children of Albion* anthology in the *New Departures/Resurgence* joint issue, characteristically conjures up the spooks of the thought-police:

> As long as the weekend reviews, Arts Council/BBC/Printing
> House Square and university conspiracies are looked up
> to as the acme of good taste and reputations, poetry and
> the arts are lost to the mercies of state-political
> control.

Quite aside from the question of their descriptive accuracy, such outbursts have an important strategic function; they help to reassure both the maligned clerisy and the rebellious stylists that neither would gain from a dialogue with the other. Moreover, they create visible orthodoxies and conspiracies out of what had before seemed only a tangle of institutions with no special sympathy for one another. If a 'literary establishment' does exist it certainly operates in subtler, possibly more insidious ways, than either Nuttall or Horovitz gives it credit for.

But does it exist at all? One way of checking is to list all the publishers acknowledged in anthologies and all the periodicals cited in individual collections. Is there a publishers' cartel or 'ring'? Which are the most important periodicals; who are their editors, reviewers, and contributors; and how often do these individual names recur? How visible are policy lines, if any, in publishers' lists and, say, a year's run of selected periodicals? Is it possible to map a career profile of a poem from its composition to its appearance in an anthology or a university course on modern literature? Could one then draw a predictive portrait of the poem-most-likely-to-succeed? A systematic research project based on these questions might turn up some extremely interesting answers; all I can do here is to offer an impressionistic sketch.

On the evidence of the anthologies and collections on my own bookshelves—the sources of all the poems in this book, except those I've quoted direct from periodicals—a handful of magazines and their editors account for a very large proportion of the initial publications of the verse I've been exploring here. If the writer was English he probably sent the poem he had written to *London Magazine*, or the B.B.C. Radio 3 programme, 'Poetry Now'; to the *New Statesman* or *The Listener* or *The Times Literary Supplement* or *Encounter*. The *Transatlantic Review* and *The Review* stand rather further behind these six major platforms, followed by magazines like *Outposts, Ambit,* and *Stand*. Both English and American writers published their poems in the high-paying American glossies; the *New Yorker, Harper's,* and *Atlantic Monthly*. Three of the American reviews recur more frequently than any others: *Hudson, Kenyon,* and *Partisan*. *Poetry (Chicago)* accounts for a very high proportion of both English and American first printings; while American little magazines, more catholic and more ubiquitous than English ones, include *Origin, Fuck You, Burning Deck, Yugen, Quagga,* and the *Journal of Creative Behaviour*. But the vast mass of cyclostyled 'mags' (with the brave English exception of Jeff Nuttall's own, now defunct, *My Own Mag*) hardly show up at all on the acknowledgments pages. I will come to them later.

The English literary situation looks, on the surface, much more amenable to conspiracy theories than does the American one. With the exception of Karl Miller, of *The Listener*, all our major literary and poetry editors are themselves practising poets: Alan Ross, George MacBeth, Anthony Thwaite, Ian Hamilton, and D. J. Enright. Indeed, three of them are represented in *The New Poetry*, edited by A. Alvarez (himself a poetry editor—of *The Observer*—and poet); the despised anti-Bible of the British Underground. And certainly there's a great deal of swapping around between journals: Ian Hamilton, editor of *The Review* and poetry editor of the T.L.S., regularly reviews in both the *New Statesman* and *The Listener*, as does Enright, of *Encounter*. The poetry reviewers of these magazines also tend to be practitioners; and both

Peter Porter and Alan Brownjohn seem to lead an almost miraculously hydra-headed literary life.

One wouldn't need to be paranoid to catch the whiff of an orthodoxy about all this; the flavour of the Oxford English school, and the London publishers' party, of a self-conscious, quizzically ironic liberalism of a kind that has, perhaps, been over-represented in recent British verse. Yet if one looks at the actual poems which these editors are printing and these reviewers are approving, there is a nervous heterodoxy of taste, a determined—and often puzzlingly generous—catholicism. The principles of selection seem to be basically negative; a desire for the 'different', the provincial, the un-discovered. So Alan Ross, in the *London Magazine*, prints, alongside Tom Pickard, Tom Raworth, and Brian Patten, all sorts of strange teenagers doing queer things in lower case. There are girl-poets in *The Listener* and poets from Hull in the *New Statesman*. On the radio programme 'Poetry Now' there is anybody and everybody. One senses, not that major talents are being excluded on some rigorous ideological loyalty-test, but that almost any talent would be welcome, given the cur-rent dearth of new poets. The multi-sided discovery of Douglas Dunn a couple of years ago was a case in point. Within around a month English readers were deluged with sharp, accurate, not over-ambitious poems by Dunn, in (at least) *London Magazine*, the *New Statesman*, and *The Listener*, followed, very shortly, by reviews by him in the same maga-zines. I don't want the example to be invidious, since I greatly admire *Terry Street*, Dunn's first collection; but I think he probably suffered from this fairly drastic over-exposure. What had happened was that he'd sent off folders of his work to a number of editors, and they'd all seized on it at once.

Poetry-reviewing in these periodicals is no more stringent. With the sole exception of Ian Hamilton, who maintains a lonely and thinly populated regime of excellence, and has, as a result, acquired a reputation more appropriate to a Central Park mugger, the general tone of verse reviews, quite unlike the hatchets which fall, paragraph by paragraph, in the fiction columns, is one of meek hospitality towards even the most obstreperous guests. The voices of Porter and Brownjohn, both of whom are often critically snappish in their own poetry, turn curiously conciliatory when they wear their reviewers' hats. A year or so ago, in a radio talk on the differences between English and American poets, Donald Davie took Porter to task for his hangdog manner in a *London Magazine* piece on Olson, Duncan, McClure, and others. The review (in the July–August 1969 issue) included these sentences:

> Any British poet setting out to criticize American
> verse had better begin by acknowledging that
> Americans write more audaciously and more commandingly
> than we do, even if he's sick of being told so by
> the Americans themselves. Nevertheless, I find it
> easy to resist the work of the five American poets
> under review, although I see much to admire and a
> great number of individual lines to enjoy.

The 'although' and 'nevertheless' are characteristic devices, brought into play at the faintest whisper of Black Mountain, or San Francisco, or the Livercastle hegemony. If the praise is meanly measured and carefully qualified, blame tends to take the form of a series of nervous, instantly retracted, smacks. The old style of English reviewing—urbane, pompous, and monstrously judicial—has, thankfully, largely disappeared; but what has taken its place leans and dodges away from making any final judgments of value at all. If a conspiracy exists in the periodicals, it seems to me more likely that there will be a plot to tolerate and include rather than, as rumour has it, to attack and exclude.

The argument works a little better at the level of the volume. Of those poets who do publish with a large commercial organization the vast majority are with Faber and Faber, Jonathan Cape, Macmillan, or the Oxford University Press.

For the publishers themselves a book of verse probably represents a sale of one to three thousand copies, at a price of only about £1. Given the cost of paper, printing and advertising, the high percentage of profit absorbed by the retail bookseller (around $33\frac{1}{3}$ per cent), and an industrial formula which hinges on making a low profit margin pay by producing in very large numbers (practically impossible for poetry, with a handful of celebrated exceptions), it's not surprising that the book of verse is often a publisher's act of charity to a potential novelist. But from the 1950s onwards poetry-publishing has moved decisively away from the big commercial firm. The Hand and Flower Press, the Fantasy Press, and the Marvell Press prefigured the rash of little presses that grew up during the 1960s: Trigram, Wild Hawthorn, Migrant, Workshop, as well as Stuart Montgomery's Fulcrum, a kind of English equivalent to the San Francisco City Lights, only with much higher standards of design and layout.

And the small press always tends to some sort of ideological coherence; its titles get published more because the proprietors like the books, or are friends with their authors, than because of the recommendations of an outside reader or the pressures of commercial interests working independently of personal taste. The small press thrives on groups and schools. Both Fulcrum and City Lights, having grown large in their time, have had an enormous influence on verse-buying and reading; between them they have given the West Coast poets, the Black Mountaineers, and some of the English writers of speech-and-place poetry an international identity. Many of their customers develop a loyalty to the taste of the press, buying more on the imprint than on the author. Consequently the press itself finds its partisan stance being endorsed by its audience. My own guess is that the proliferation of poetic styles over the last ten years or so has been enabled and accelerated by the small press; but when publishing is decentralized into such guerrilla units the necessity for dialogue and argument drops away. Small eccentric voices are able to swell into oracles in tiny, besotted communities of like minds. Indeed, the sad hallmarks of the really small press and the roneo'd mag are invariably megalomania and solipsism.

Though this is, perhaps, a touch unfair, since one of their central avowed functions is to devote themselves to the publishing of what they believe to be bad verse. Jeff Nuttall again:

> All over Europe, America, then, artists, creative people,
> stepped aside into a deliberate sell-it-yourself amateurism.
> This was the beginning of the Underground . . . Since 1956
> City Lights had shown what could happen if you ignored
> the professional middlemen and set up in business yourself.
> You immediately got all the profit, sidestepped the critics,
> and were your own censor. The most intolerable stuff got
> to be published—at last. At long long last 'standards'
> went to the wind.

One knows exactly what he means. The overwhelming impression of the duplicated little magazine, probably run off in the back room of a bookshop, with smudgy ink and loose staples, is of temporaneity and badness of a thoroughly deliberate kind. The work they present bears no more relation to impersonal standards of poetic excellence than primary-school music-and-movement classes do to the Royal Ballet Company. The context offered by the mag is an opportunity to be yourself, to mess about, to play. Two examples here, taken, more or less at random, from mags called 'Cosmos' and 'Norch':

> World peace;
> Or is it the morphic faint of a prostitute?
> Ashes of sexocide hover over the generation
> Once again hungry roots/re spreading into my abdomen, i/m
>   using
> This civilization like a lavatory of the Sealdah Rail-Station
> Life uses me
> & is pushing me towards a scentless babyearth
> POLICE & URINE

Shala of the brown eyes.
   yes brown pool clear mud does not cry at knowledge
   knows more than wide seas proud stags sunny wise lovers
   is there
   her smile does not speak
                    it smiles
   her lips are of lip and also sky yellow birds
   talking wholly of nothing on their tightrope
   and then down up up and shies away
                       day
   brakes precisely eighteen seconds from now
   and the night gives up more honorably than the day
                   fading over the curve
   ho   ho
   chortles the hedgehog safely on land
   if I had wings I would not be a hedgehog

The most interesting thing about both of these is that they are conspicuously not trying to be poems; it's enough to swear or doodle—quite unlike the strained pastiches which occupy the bulk of most university literary magazines. They justly resent 'criticism' and 'standards', since such things are wholly irrelevant to the essentially social and therapeutic functions of the mag.

But there is a more unpleasant comedy in all this. While the reviled 'establishment' leans over backwards to accommodate the oddest and tiniest outbursts as real poems, the Underground scene in the mags has to get more and more consciously bad in order to escape formal adoption. We are moving ever nearer to a charade in which editors, publishers, and critics reverently follow on the heels of infants who only want the freedom to be naughty and themselves. There is a perplexing absurdity about the way in which the big commercial publishers and distribution systems are being harnessed into promoting a product whose basic nature is to be local, ephemeral, and unprofitable. The documentary interest of *The Children of Albion* anthology is undeniable, but its presentation, by Horovitz and Penguin Books, as a literary rather than a social milestone, is quite unfathomable. 'These are the energies,' says the blurb of the book, 'which have almost completely dispelled the arid critical climate of the fifties and engineered a fresh renaissance of "the voice of the Bard".' But the whole point of the Underground ethic—made sympathetically plain by Nuttall in *Bomb Culture*—is that it does not dispel, nor does it engineer; our new-style Huck Finns are contemptuous of any such essentially transitive relationships with either external society or literary tradition.

To my mind, the most depressing signal of this confusion between verse-as-written and its systems of transmission is the recent emergence of the best-selling rebel poet. The marketing campaigns that have been mounted round Leonard Cohen and Rod Mc Kuen are staggeringly at odds with their soggy, artless, deliberately shambling lyrics; the professional hard-sell is used to promote the notion of the amateur, the drop-out, the underground. The indulgence of the mag is itself turned into a packageable commodity. Cohen's verses, for instance, are cosmetic concoctions in which the romantic furniture of a Sinatra song is dusted with a few contemporary references, and aimless, mechanical paradoxes add the illusion of 'depth'. Allusions to war, drugs, the *I Ching* and astrology, sex and death, scattered piecemeal, pass for prophetic urgency. There is an equal affection for incantatory bombast and a kind of vagueness which, if not inspected too closely, might be mistaken for surrealism.

> Come to me if you grow old
> come to me if you need coffee
>
> Suzanne takes your hand
> and she leads you to the river,
> she is wearing rags and feathers
> from Salvation Army counters.
> The sun pours down like honey
> on our lady of the harbour
> as she shows you where to look

among the garbage and the flowers,
there are heroes in the seaweed . . .

I see you on a Greek mattress
reading the *Book of Changes*,
Lebanese candy in the air.
On the whitewashed wall I see
you raise another hexagram
for the same old question:
how can you be free?

They come, perhaps, a little too pat for genuine mag offerings,
but the verbal devices Cohen uses are all toys of the kind one
finds in the play-poems of the Underground; slicked up for
mass consumption. Yet Cohen's *Poems: 1956–1968* was one
of the initial titles with which Jonathan Cape—probably the
most enterprising and committed of all large publishers—
launched their new series of *Cape Poetry Paperbacks*. There is
at present a basic, nervous uncertainty of taste and judgment
which is chronically affecting the way in which poetry is
being sold, read, and, ultimately, written.

One can see all sorts of good reasons why this uncertainty—
which manifests itself most frequently as a style of manic
hospitality—should exist. The break-up of a working consensus, a cultural centre, has led to a provincialization of
experience—to the adoption of extreme, isolationist attitudes.
The old values of literary culture have been hastily abandoned
as we've all rushed to stand, in line, along extremity's
millennial brink. The surrounding climate of continuous
change has encouraged experiments with means and processes much more than it has allowed any sort of assessment of
the worth and purpose of the objects we produce. Cultural
decentralization has meant that even such basic communicative instruments as the printing-press have gone into the
eccentric attics and back-gardens of society; from where they
issue often illegible missives, printed in a blotchy, possibly
astral, code.

But these are only reasons, and we have a good deal to fear

from them. They have made contemporary poetry extra-ordinary difficult to see at all clearly. Too often they have forced both poets and critics into absurdly opposing camps; reactionaries versus enthusiasts. More and more, poets are not entering into any sort of dialogue about their work. The old war of the bards against the reviewers has opened up even more furiously; poets writing about critics tend nowadays to take the line that all critics are either your worst enemies or your blurb-writers, and that it's pointless to argue the toss anywhere in between those extremes. What we need now, much more than the most daring experiment in anti-language and post-poetry, is a vocabulary for discriminating seriously between some poems and others; a language of preference and value. For without it our literature is in serious danger of turning into an enormous and varied repertoire of tricks, contortions, and balancing acts; a treasure-trove of entertaining gadgets. The society of the poem is already showing signs of being a Mad Hatter's tea-party of nutty inventors.

Book List

This is a personal list of books I've gone to most often while I was writing. The individual collections, which are listed under their author's names, aren't the only work, nor necessarily the most recent, of that particular poet; they are the ones which either seemed most relevant to my argument, or, as often as not, the ones which just happened to be around. My list, like my book, reflects the vagaries of my own bookshelves. I pillaged from anthologies a great deal, and I imagine the book being read in conjunction with some, at least, of the anthologies listed here.

1. ANTHOLOGIES OF RECENT POETRY

The New American Poetry, edited by DONALD M. ALLEN (New York and London, 1960).

The New Writing in the USA, edited by DONALD M. ALLEN and ROBERT CREELEY (London, 1967).

The New Poetry, edited by A. ALVAREZ (London, 1962; revised edition, 1966).

The Poetry of Rock, edited by RICHARD GOLDSTEIN (New York and London, 1969).

Children of Albion: Poetry of the 'Underground' in Britain, edited by MICHAEL HOROVITZ (London, 1969).

British Poetry since 1945, edited by EDWARD LUCIE-SMITH (London, 1970).

Concrete Poetry, edited by EMMETT WILLIAMS (London, 1967).

The *Penguin Modern Poetry*, series, Nos. 1–14, have also provided a continuously expanding anthology of British verse, with American poets also making some erratic appearances in occasional issues.

2. INDIVIDUAL COLLECTIONS

BERRYMAN, JOHN: *77 Dream Songs* (New York and London, 1964).

MACBETH, GEORGE: *The Night of Stones* (London, 1968).
———————   *The Burning Cone* (London, 1970).

BROWNJOHN, ALAN: *Sandgrains on a Tray* (London, 1969).

COHEN, LEONARD: *Poems 1956–1968* (London, 1969).

CREELEY, ROBERT: *Poems 1950–1965* (London, 1966).

DORN, EDWARD: *The North Atlantic Turbine* (London, 1967).
———————   *Gunslinger 1 & 2* (London, 1970).

DUNCAN, ROBERT: *The Opening of the Field* (New York, 1960).

FINLAY, IAN HAMILTON: *The Dancers Inherit the Party*
                              (London, 1961 and 1969).

GINSBERG, ALLEN: *Kaddish* (San Francisco, 1961).
———————   *Planet News* (San Francisco, 1969).

HENRI, ADRIAN: *Tonight at Noon* (London, 1968).

HUGHES, TED: *Wodwo* (London, 1967).
———————   *Crow* (London, 1970).

LARKIN, PHILIP: *The Less Deceived* (Hessle, 1955).
———————   *The Whitsun Weddings* (London, 1964).

LOWELL, ROBERT: *For the Union Dead* (London, 1964).
———————   *Selected Poems* (London, 1965).
———————   *Notebook* (London, 1970).

MIDDLETON, CHRISTOPHER: *Our Flowers & Nice Bones*
                              (London, 1969).

MITCHELL, ADRIAN: *Poems* (London, 1969).

MORGAN, EDWIN: *The Second Life* (Edinburgh, 1968).

OLSON, CHARLES: *The Maximus Poems* (New York, 1960).
———————   *Maximus Poems IV, V, VI* (London, 1969).

PATTEN, BRIAN: *Notes to the Hurrying Man* (London, 1969).

PLATH, SYLVIA: *Ariel* (London, 1965).

PORTER, PETER: *A Porter Folio* (London, 1969).
———————— *The Last of England* (London, 1970).

RAWORTH, TOM: *The Relation Ship* (London, 1967).

SNODGRASS, W. D.: *Heart's Needle* (New York, 1959).
———————— *After Experience* (London, 1968).

SNYDER, GARY: *Collected Poems* (London, 1966).
———————— *Six Sections from Mountains and Rivers without End* (London, 1967).

TOMLINSON, CHARLES: *American Scenes* (London, 1966).
———————— *The Way of a World* (London, 1969).

UPDIKE, JOHN: *Midpoint* (London, 1969).

Acknowledgments

For their kind permission to reprint the extracts of poetry in this book thanks are due to the following poets and publishers:

W H AUDEN 'The Poet and the City', *The Dyer's Hand*; 'Musée des Beaux Arts' *Collected Shorter Poems 1927–57*; the extract on p 67 from 'Whitsunday in Kirchstetter' *About the House*. All published by Faber & Faber

ROLAND BARTHES *Writing Degree Zero*, translated by Dr Annette Lavers and Dr Colin Smith, Cape Editions, Jonathan Cape

JORGE LUIS BORGES 'Borges and I' *Labyrinths* Penguin Modern Classics

ALAN BROWNJOHN 'A 202', 'Balls of Sweetness' *Sandgrains on a Tray* Macmillan

LEONARD COHEN 'Suzanne', 'I see you on a Greek mattress' *Selected Poems* Jonathan Cape

ROBERT CREELEY 'Hello' *Poems 1960–1965* Calder & Boyars

DONALD DAVIE *First Epistle to Eva Hesse* London Magazine Editions

EDWARD DORN 'Oxford' *The North Atlantic Turbine*; *Gunslinger 1 & 2* Fulcrum Press

T S ELIOT 'The Love Song of J Alfred Prufrock', 'A Cooking Egg' *Selected Poems*; *The Waste Land* Faber & Faber

IAN HAMILTON FINLAY 'Catch' *The Dancers Inherit the Party* Fulcrum Press; 'Acrobat' The Times Literary Supplement (No 3, 258)

ALLEN GINSBERG 'The Change: Kyoto-Tokyo Express' *Planet News* City Lights Books

ADRIAN HENRI 'Poem in Memoriam T S Eliot'; 'I Want to Paint', *Tonight at Noon* Rapp & Whiting

DOM SYLVESTER HOUEDARD *Plakat 1* Openings Press

TED HUGHES *Crow* Faber & Faber

PHILIP LARKIN 'Mr Bleaney' *The Whitsun Weddings* Faber & Faber

GEORGE MACBETH 'The Painter's Model' London Magazine

ROBERT LOWELL *Notebook* Faber & Faber

ROGER McGOUGH 'Aren't We All' *The Mersey Sound* Penguin Modern Poets 10

CHRISTOPHER MIDDLETON 'Computer's Karl Marx', 'The Joke' *Our Flowers and Nice Bones* Fulcrum Press

STUART MILLS 'The Sea is . . . .' London Magazine Editions

ADRIAN MITCHELL 'Order Me A Transparent Coffin And Dig My Crazy Grave', 'Man at Large' *Poems* Jonathan Cape

EDWIN MORGAN 'Il faut être absolument moderne' *Starry-veldt* Eugene Gomringer, Erkersreuth; 'Opening the Cage' *The Second Life* Edinburgh University Press

JEFF NUTTALL *Bomb Culture* MacGibbon & Kee

CHARLES OLSON *The Maximus Poems* Cape Goliard

BRIAN PATTEN 'Schoolboy' *Little Johnny's Confession* Allen & Unwin

TOM PICKARD 'Shag', 'Bunk' London Magazine

SYLVIA PLATH 'Daddy' *Ariel* Faber & Faber, by permission of Miss Olwyn Hughes

PETER PORTER 'Your Attention Please' *Once Bitten Twice Bitten* Scorpion Press; 'Short Story', 'Europe' *The Last of England* Oxford University Press

EZRA POUND *Selected Cantos* Faber & Faber

TOM RAWORTH 'You Were Wearing Blue' *The Relation Ship* Cape Goliard

TADEUSZ RÓZEWICZ 'My Poetry', 'Pigtail' *Faces of Anxiety* translated by Adam Czerniawski, Rapp & Whiting

W D SNODGRASS 'Autumn Scene', 'Regraduating the Lute', 'Reconstructions' *After Experience* Oxford University Press; 'April Inventory' *Heart's Needle* Marvell Press

GARY SNYDER 'Bubb's Creek Haircut' *Six Sections from Mountains and Rivers Without End* Fulcrum Press

WALLACE STEVENS 'Credences of Summer', 'Notes Toward

a Supreme Fiction' *The Collected Poems of Wallace Stevens*; 'Adagia' *Opus Posthumus*, Faber & Faber.

R S THOMAS 'Walter Llywach' *Tares* Rupert Hart-Davies

CHARLES TOMLINSON 'The Chances of Rhyme', 'Prometheus', 'Descartes and the Stove', Swimming Chenango Lake', 'Terminal Tramps' *The Way of a World* Oxford University Press.

DAVID TRIBE 'Empty Skies' Tribune, Nov 1970

JOHN UPDIKE *Midpoint* Andre Deutsch

HUGO WILLIAMS 'The Couple Upstairs' *Sugar Daddy* Oxford University Press

WILLIAM CARLOS WILLIAMS *Paterson* MacGibbon & Kee, New Directions NY